The Layers of Our Seeing

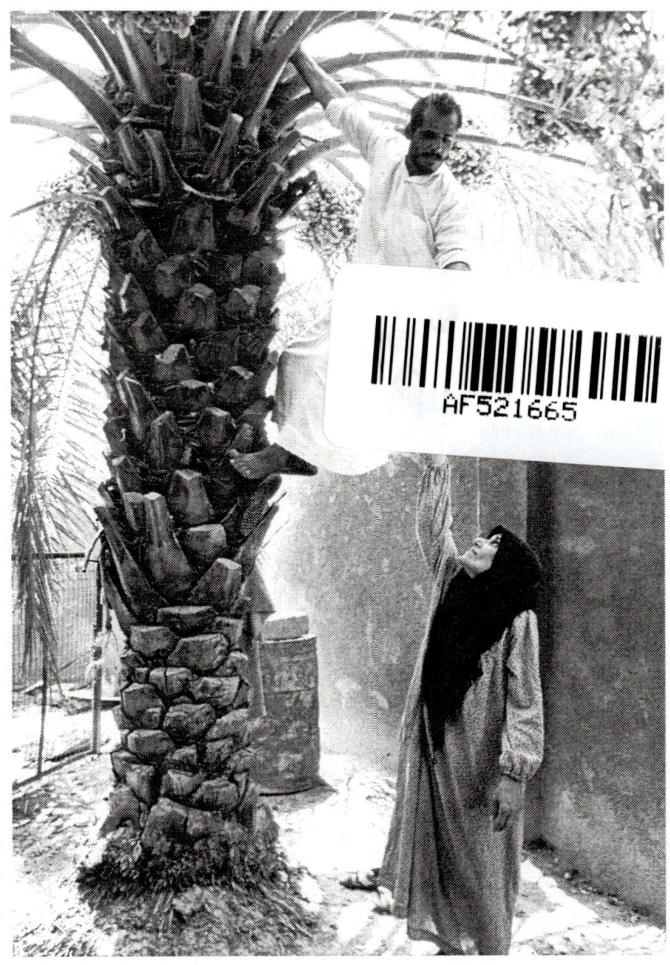

Susan Bright, Muna Hamzeh
and Alan Pogue

Plain View Press
P. O. 33311
Austin, TX 78764

plainviewpress.com
sbright1@austin.rr.com
1-800-878-3605

ISBN: 1-891386-27-1
Library of Congress Number: 2001099049

Cover and Title Page Photograph:
Gathering Dates, Basra, 2000
Iraqi couple gathers dates for their guests in their courtyard. It was 128 degrees in August. I was collapsing from the heat so they poured a pitcher of cold water over my head and gathered dates so I could have some sugar. Iraq was the largest exporter of dates in the world before the gulf war blew up so many of their trees.

Thanks

from Susan

Thanks to Glee Ingram for editing and helping me shape this and all my books. Thanks to Sarah Bolz for editorial and proof reading help and for all she has done for Plain View Press. Thanks to Lauren Carrozzi for proof reading. Thanks to my family for giving me time and space and a free environment in which to work.

from Alan

Thanks to the American Friends Service Committee, Voices in the Wilderness and Veterans for Peace for facilitating my trips to the Middle East.

from Muna

Thanks to all the friends I've made in Austin who have shown me, each and every one, that there are Americans who care.

The people of the earth must make a peace too strong for leaders to resist.

Alan Pogue

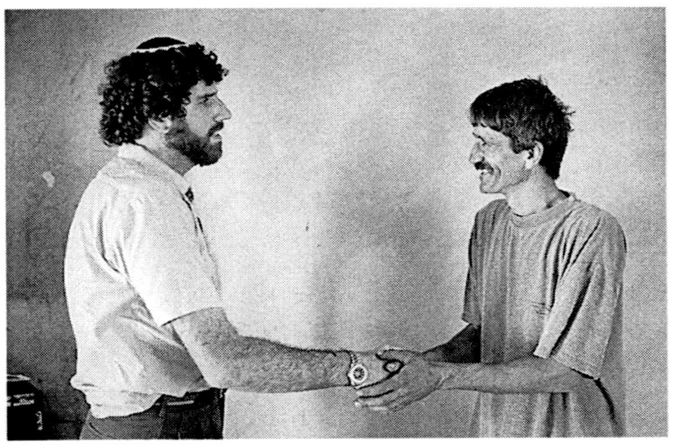

Touching Peace, Hebron, 2001. *Rabbi Arik Ascherman, co-director of Rabbis for Human Rights, shakes the hand of Atta Jabber, a Palestinian farmer who has received a home demolition order from the Israeli army. Rabbi Ascherman has travelled from Jerusalem to give his moral support to Atta and his family. The extended Jabber family has endured thirteen property demolitions. Rabbis for Human Rights is the only organization of Jewish Rabbis to include members of all Jewish traditional religious groups. Like most peace groups, they are against the occupation of Palestine and they support Jerusalem being the joint capital of the two states.*

AP

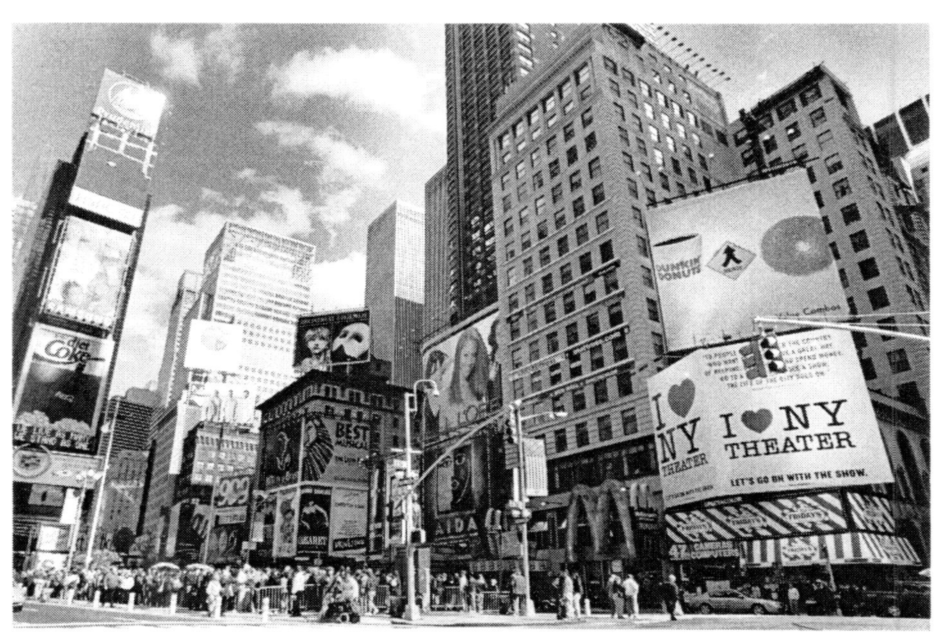

On With the Show, New York City, 2001.

People waiting for theater tickets October 9, 2001. New Yorkers flocked to see *Les Miserables*. I was there attending an international conference on prison reform.

Introduction

The Wednesday after the Sunday when the U.S. began bombing Afghanistan, I was standing next to Susan Bright in the Women in Black vigil at the South Gate of the Texas Capitol building in Austin, Texas. We had been meeting like this weekly at noon since shortly after the airplanes hit the Pentagon and the World Trade Center; women wearing black standing for peace, projecting our heartfelt advice against overreaction. As time passed without Bush ordering a military strike on that captive country Afghanistan, I at least had dared to hope. Maybe the national grief would resolve in common sense responses and measured justice, and not a wildfire of vengeance. Maybe losing our own innocent civilians in something Bush had termed "an act of war" would give our nation empathy for innocent civilians abroad.

Now it was too late for prevention. What remained of the infrastructure of Kabul and other cities was being hammered with deadly annihilative force. Every person capable of motion was trying to flee Afghanistan across closed borders of neighboring countries. U.N. feeding programs had been suspended because of the bombing. The U.S. was dropping enough odd little meal packets for a few tens of thousands of people while millions were hungry. Some of the air-dropped things were smashing on impact, we had heard, and others landed temptingly in mine fields.

I cried when I heard. I thought about a poem Susan had written. She called it "Soft Bombs." Come to my kitchen, I invited her, let me interview you for the radio, read me your poems. Political speech seems to have failed, I said, we need heart speech. So she came over and we drank tea and she read to me across the kitchen table. She read "Soft Bombs" and "Fly Naked," and other topical poems, including "Enheduanna Wrote on Stone," an older poem I requested, which I had aired in my radio newscast back in 1991 when Bush *pere* was bombing Iraq. The audience loved them. One woman called up and said she wanted "Soft Bombs" to be on the radio every day.

What I like so much about "Soft Bombs" is the relentlessness. As it keeps naming and naming all the kinds of things that people in Afghanistan must need, so many things that we ourselves cherish and take for granted, the chasm between our situation and theirs becomes more and more apparent. And through the list of their needs, their human similarity to ourselves is built in loving, overwhelming detail.

The human reality of people who have been alienated from us by politics, war, and demonization, is very much the keynote of this book. Susan told me that when she saw the photos Alan Pogue had taken in Iraq, she felt so connected to the people that she wanted to write about them.

You who take this book in your hand may perhaps live far away from us in Austin, Texas. That's as it should be. But as the introducer, it behooves me to say that Susan Bright and Alan Pogue have long been human treasures of this city. They are among our best-loved artist-soothsayers. Since the '70s and '60s, respectively, they have been relentless in showing and telling us things we need to know, in order to not become complacent in our town's self-denomination as the "Live Music Capital of the World." Here they are joined by newcomer Muna Hamzeh, whose vivid writing has also brought the town to its feet.

Muna is a Palestinian American journalist who has settled in Austin after living for a decade in the Dheisheh Refugee Camp in Bethlehem where she grew to know the lives, hearts, and trials of a people trapped in a half century long conflict. As a Jewish American, I am grateful for the chance to read her, and happy to know she, I, and Susan, each from a different background, have stood shoulder to shoulder doing Women in Black in Austin, as Palestinian and Jewish Israelis do in Israel, and Bosnians and Serbs in former Yugoslavia.

This book by Susan, Alan, and Muna says with art in an enduring way the things we try to say with our bodies in the one-hour vigils: There are humans like us under the falling bombs. Feel them. See them. Be them. Know that choosing peace is more sane than choosing sides. The book pokes holes in constructs that prevent people from seeing others' reality. As Susan writes in the first poem, and Alan's photo shows:

"If I look /through this hole /at the world /and understand it, /nothing will/ ever look the same/ to me again."

Frieda Werden, December 9, 2001.
Radio Producer, WINGS: Women's International
News Gathering Service, www.wings.org

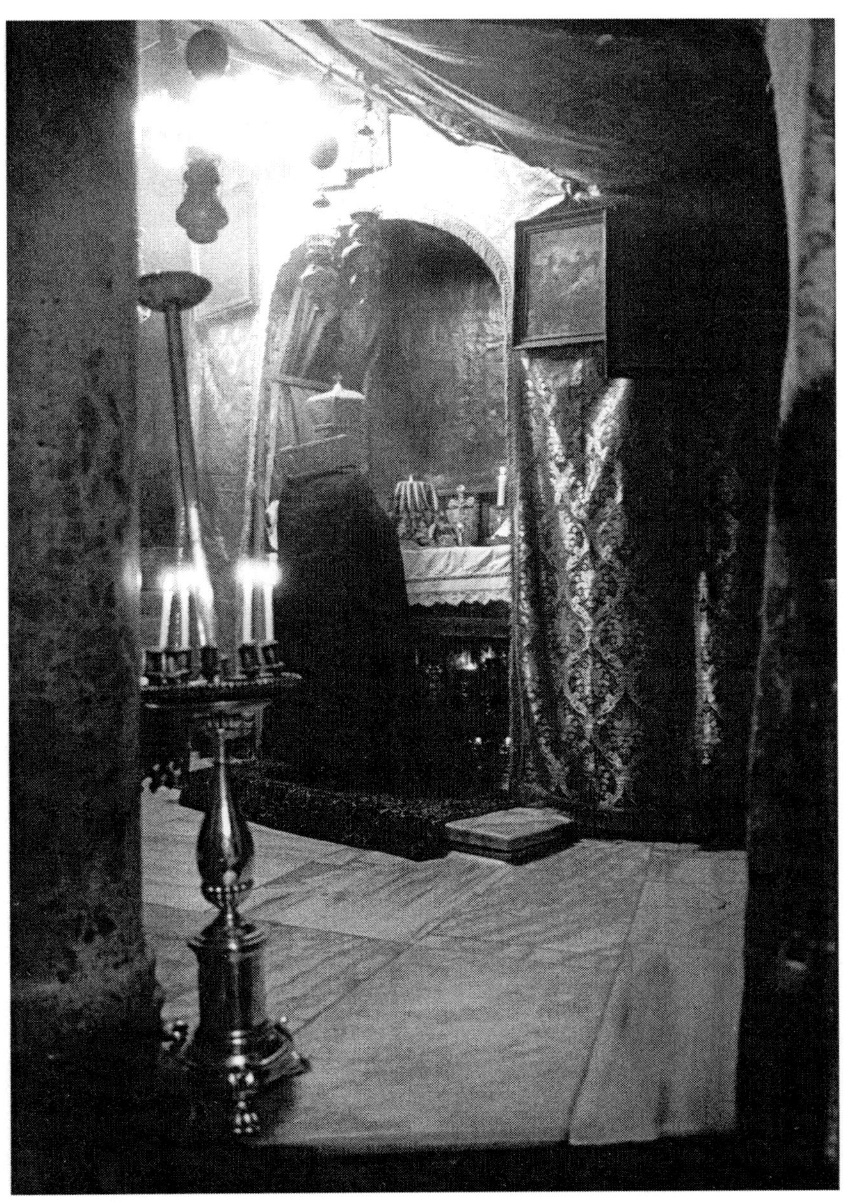

Altar of the Nativity, Bethlehem, 2001. *This altar is below ground level over the place Jesus Christ was born. Four religious orders share the present church, which is now part of Palestine: Greek Orthodox, Franciscans, Armenian Orthodox and Roman Catholics. Below the altar on the floor is a star with a hole in the middle through which one can look down to the original birth place. Further down a cave-like passage is the room in which St. Jerome translated the bible from Greek to the Latin Vulgate so common people could read it. The ground level door to the church was made four feet high, too low for soldiers to ride their horses into the holy place.*

Hole

If I look
through this hole
at Gilo
across the ditch —
a village made of
mud blocks baked
in hot light,
the first thing
I know
is that something
is wrong.

The hole
is not supposed to exist
and then,
because of the light,
I know
there's no roof —
so the wall
and this hole
are what remains
of a structure
that was intended
to shelter
human
beings.

If I look
through this hole
at the world
and understand it,
nothing will
ever look the same
to me again.

SB

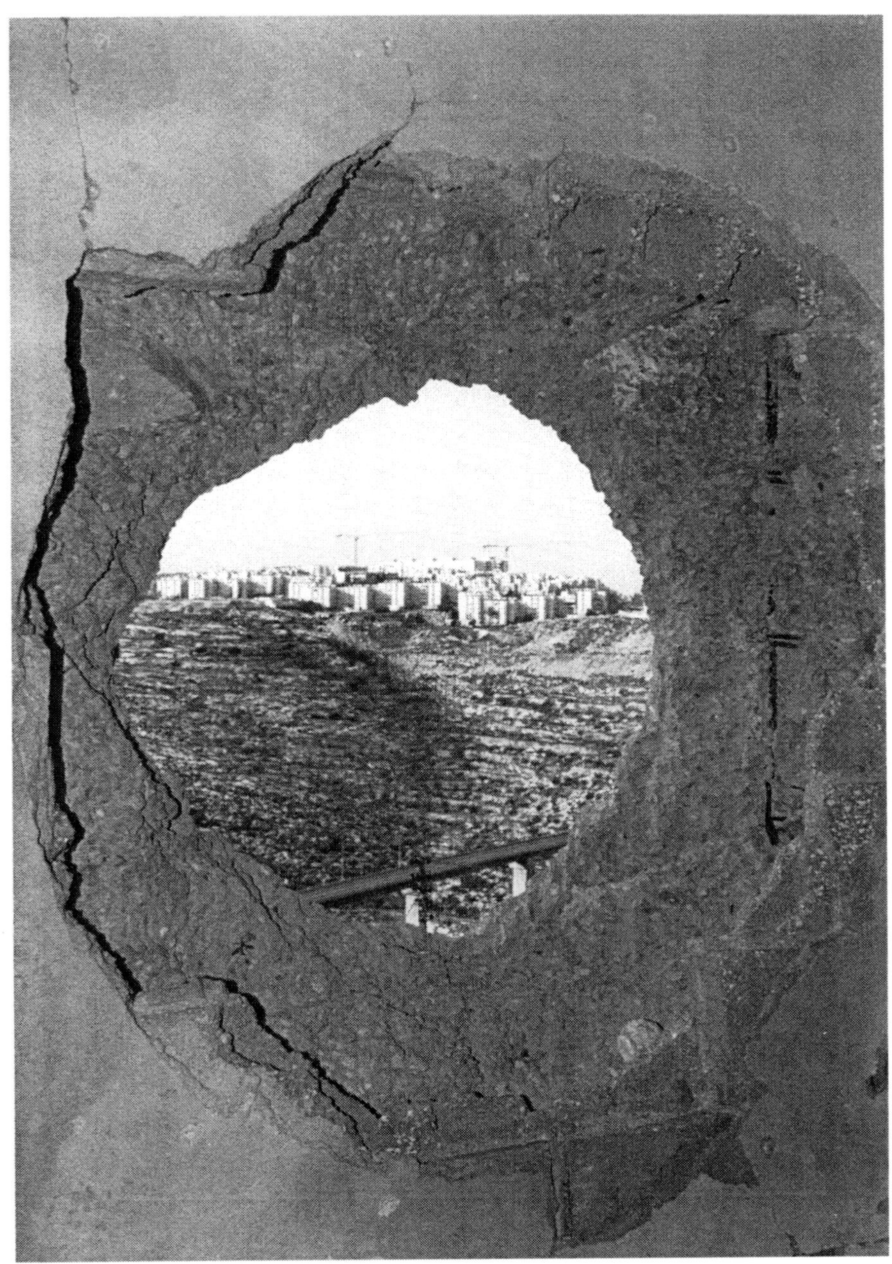

View from Bethlehem, Palestine, the Middle East, 2001.

The hole in the wall is in a house in Beit Jala, a small quaint town next to Bethlehem that has been heavily bombarded by the Israeli military in the past year. Through the hole one can see Gilo, a very large Israeli settlement built on confiscated Palestinian land. *AP*

Contents

Soft Bombs

Fill airplanes and helicopters, trucks and the cargo space on the backs of donkeys with food and medicine. Airlift tents and blankets, fly in some cows and bales of hay. Fly in books and radios, justice and hope. Drop feather beds and pillows, down coats in every size. Send mirrors wrapped in bubble wrap so the women can see themselves — how beautiful they are. Send butter and olive oil, garlic and beans. Bomb them with soft tacos. Fly in flowers. Drop them by the thousands, and chocolate, milk and more milk. Float down boxes full of chickens laying eggs and sheep and goats and animal feed. Send in foster parents for children who have nobody to take care of them. Drop teddy bears and dolls. Send crayons and notebooks. Send alphabet primers in Pashtun and all the languages the people of Afghanistan speak. Send laptop computers with translation programs and internet connections to circumvent the patriarchy. Send generators and cell phones with satellite connections. Send in televisions and video cams, tape recorders, batteries and chargers. Send medicine to get rid of lice, antibiotics, soap, clean clothing, shoes and hats, canes, gloves, boots, rain gear, down comforters, charcoal to build fires, matches, water purification tablets. Airlift bottled water, not for soldiers, but for people, and lumber to build shelter. Send letters from Afghan refugees all over the world who want to know how their friends and family are, who are a great Diaspora full of love and concern. Send airplane tickets to anyplace people want to go, quickly before winter sets in and people freeze to death. Bomb the people of Afghanistan with soft things to wrap around their bodies, food to keep them alive and then set up schools and universities. Follow these soft bombs with administrations of social workers, carpenters, doctors, teachers, civil servants, engineers who can help Afghans rebuild the infrastructure of a land that has already been bombed with back to the stone age. Then ask the people of Afghanistan to turn terrorists from their midst, after they have food in their bellies and roofs over their heads, when children are strong and laughing, when the sports arena in Kabul is used for soccer and not massacre. Drop lipstick and long underwear. Bomb the people of Afghanistan with soft bombs, things that give life and justice and hope. Bomb them with diversity and tolerance, creativity and goodwill because the other way doesn't work, because there have to be alternatives. Air lift bullet proof vests and helmets. Send soldiers to protect journalists, doctors, relief workers, truck loads of humanitarian aid and wheat. Send soldiers to refugee camps to protect civilians from disaster.

SB

Alphabet

It is sixA.M.
A child
is writing, carefully,
the alphabet
in her notebook.

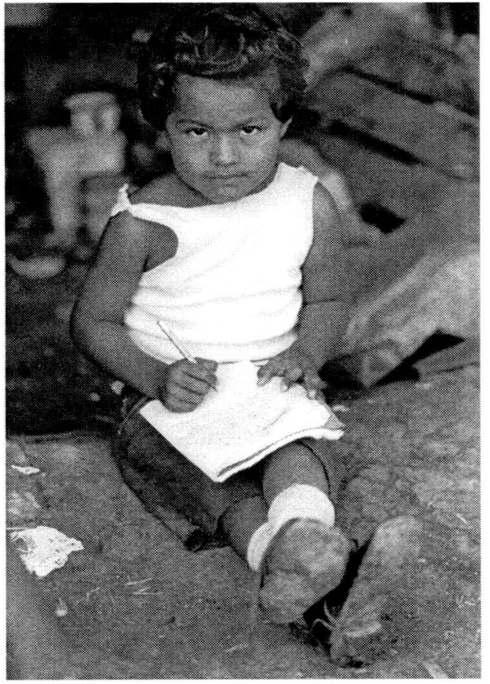

If there were 100 people
in the world —
53 would be female,
58 would be under 25 years old
70 would be people of color
70 would be non-Christian
58 would be Asian/Pacific
21 would be Africans
21 would be Europeans
14 of those would live in
the Americas, North and South
80 would live in poverty
50 of those would be women
70 would be illiterate
50 of whom would be women
50 would be starving or malnourished
6 would own 59% of the world's wealth
one would own a computer
one would have a college education —
these two would both be
from the United States. *

If 100 civilians
inhabited a war zone during
World War I,
5 would die of war,
in World War II,
50 would die.
In the 1990's
80 would be killed.

Continued

SB, AP

In the year 2001
90 percent
of all refugees and
displaced persons are
women and children.

The United States,
which has 3 %
of the world oil supply,
consumes 25% of it.

It is six A.M.
A child
is writing, carefully,
the alphabet
in her notebook.

She does not know these
things —

but she will.

**Some of these statistics are paraphrased from a public letter entitled "Redefining Normal," September 25, 2001, by Robin Morgan.*

(photograph preceding page)

Niña de Palito Blanco, 1981.

At dawn this child writes the alphabet over and over in a tablet while her parents prepare breakfast in Palito Blanco, Mexico. This is an encampment of three hundred people who have come together to form a cooperative on land that should have been theirs. After three years of being driven off the land repeatedly they were granted five square miles to farm.

SB, AP

Lara

Lara had seven brothers and sisters. Her father was a mean and cruel man who enjoyed beating and humiliating his children. I hated him and wished someone would come and take him away for good. But nobody ever did. His wife was a spineless woman who didn't dare leave him, kept bearing him children and was constantly beaten by him too. I resented her weakness.

One day when Lara was ten, she mustered enough courage to ask her father for 23 cents, the cost of a new notebook that her teacher at school asked her to buy. But her father wouldn't give her the money and when she cried, he knocked her around with his fists. Undeterred, Lara waited for him to leave the house, and then she crawled into the locked garage through a small opening in the wall. Her father kept all the non-perishable food locked in the garage to prevent his children from eating it. The hole was so tiny that Lara was stuck several times before she finally managed to crawl all the way through. Her mother stood in the background, threatening to tell her father when he returned. But Lara didn't care. She took one can of corned beef and crawled back out of the garage. Hiding the can under her shirt, she raced to a nearby store and sold the can for 50 cents.

On her way to school the following morning, she bought a notepad for 23 cents and a falafel sandwich with the rest of the money. She smiled to herself all day. But by evening, her youngest brother had told on her, and her painful screams filled the air as her father beat her with a metal rod on every part of her body. The next morning, she was barely able to walk to school. Her arms, legs and back were covered with black and blue bruises. A month later, Lara crawled into the garage again. She took another can of corned beef and sold it for 50 cents. This time, she bought two pink pencils and a blue eraser shaped like a flower.

When Lara turned 14, her father took her out of school and married her to a man 13 years her senior. In her new home, Lara was beaten both by her husband and by her mother-in-law. They thought her lazy for not washing the clothes fast enough, or sweeping the floors fast enough, or baking the bread fast enough. Then one day, Lara ran away and returned to her family. She was divorced by the time she turned 17. Her father stopped beating her and for that Lara was grateful. She spent her days cleaning house and tending to her younger siblings, including her newborn baby sister.

Continued

One day, Lara's baby sister was not a baby anymore. She was old enough to go to school. On a rainy December afternoon, the little girl dared ask her father for money to buy a notebook, and this was when Lara taught her how to crawl inside the locked garage.

MH

❍❍❍

You Can't Label Me

The first time I became aware that my skin had color was in Moses Lake, Washington. I was 18. Someone at college, a white American, asked me what it felt like to have dark skin. I didn't know my skin was dark. I went home after class, took off all my clothes and stared at my image in the mirror. My darkness eluded me. I couldn't find it. All I saw was a naked, female human body.

May came and the sun became blistering hot. My tan became gorgeous. I could see the envy in the eyes of those who turned lobster red when they bore their skin to the sun. I went home after class, took off my life clothes and looked in the mirror. My beautifully tanned olive skin stared back at me. I was so darn lucky to be an Arab. It felt great to have dark skin.

Someone else asked me if all Arabs lived in tents back in "Arabia." I told him that I was born in a tent. He believed me. So I told him that my dad had to ride to the next village on camel-back to announce my birth. He believed me.

Someone else asked me if all Palestinians are terrorists. I told him that we are all weaned on hand grenades and machine guns. He believed me.

MH

There Must Be Another Way

Each day my mind and soul fill up with questions. There have been
events that changed how I think about the world — the Vietnam Street
Execution, Kent State, the Poor People's Campaign.

America is engaged. We must reach out of what we think we know.
Nationalism is less important than humanity. The sky is empty.
We mourn. We mourn. I must ask —

Will the new power balance be about secret police and terrorists?
Are we embarking on the greatest witch hunt in history?
I cannot imagine losing the freedoms which make America important.

Will it happen before I get my mind around the meaning of it?
Red and black triangle hats, beards and mustaches — an inquisition
lies in the throes of birth.

I know almost nothing about Muslim culture but I like people
I meet from the Middle East. Mohammed advocated tolerance.
How can we know each other more effectively?

Once, after a long week of rain that deposited thirty feet of water
in downtown Austin, Jay and I went fishing on a lake, the top of which
was thirty feet higher than it had been the week before —

Wind blew in shivers across a water skin of turbid glass. I couldn't shake
the idea that we would fall through. Landmarks were under water,
houses on the bluff were wildly out of place.

The personal and the political veer wildly apart. Today a radical agenda
has usurped the peace movement. I send out a plea! *Please, one thing
at a time*. We must *be* peace, not *fight* for it, not *kill* for it.

There is a silent grace about it — honest veracity, deep listening.
It's back to the stone age of our minds unless we engage
in a great debate with the entire world to invent a better way.

SB

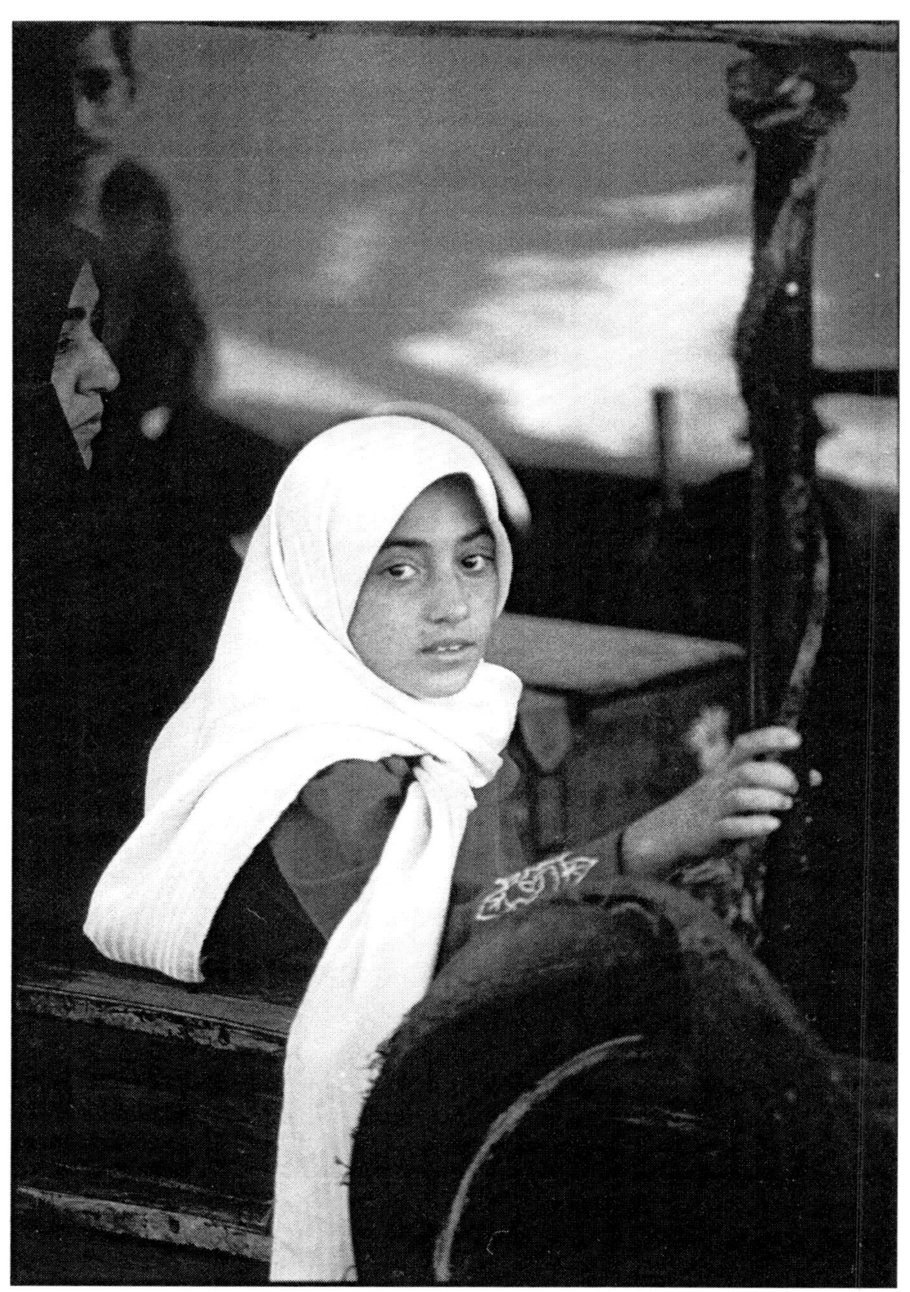

Girl in a Water Taxi
Basra, 1998.
A young girl rides along one of the tributaries of the Shatt al Arab.

AP

Enheduanna Wrote on Stone

"Born ca. 2300 B.C., Enheduanna was a moon priestess, daughter of King Sargon of Agade, who reigned over the world's first empire, extending from the Mediterranean to Persia. Enheduanna is the first writer, male or female, in history whose name and work have been preserved. Her personal history survives in highly political poems. We have a stone disk which contains a detailed likeness of the high priestess, revealing her particular features and dress, flanked by three of her retainers. The poetry we have has been preserved on cuneiform tablets." Quotation above and within text are taken from adaptations by Aliki and Willis Barnstone of "The Exaltation of Inanna," Yale Univ. Press, 1968 by William W. Hallo and J.J. A Van Dijk.

Enheduanna wrote on stone.
The first poet in recorded history was a woman
who wrote political poetry, a woman who gathered symbols,
mysterious and strange for us to see, a woman
who cut clay glyphs in order to catch thought—
cut stone words to throw at the goddess—
How dull and heavy the medium, sculpture
to chase fleet passages of mind, heartbeat—

She said:
Like a dragon you have filled the land with venom.
Like thunder when you roar over the earth,
trees and plants fall before you.
You are a flood descending from a mountain,
O primary one,
Moon Goddess Inanna of heaven and earth!
Your fire blows about and drops on our nation,
Lady mounted on a beast.
An gives you these qualities, holy commands,
but you decide.
You are in all our great rites.
Who can understand you?

Enheduanna wrote on stone,
questions about divinity and human suffering,
questions about the vibrant green of spring,
the black green of thunder, the violent green
of torrent, mountain emptying into ocean,
wars so violent earth trembled —

Continued

She said:

Storms lend you winds, destroyer of the lands.
For you the rivers rise high with blood
and the people have nothing to drink.
The army of the mountain goes to you captive
of its own accord.

Her stone words fall out of history, pour and tumble,
rough and fierce, into our lives.
It has always been so.
I have been singing this song for so long
my tongue grows thick, numb, cold and sullen,
snake hair, stone face, over and over,
since there were words
we have used them to unmask savage gods.

She said:

You have lifted your foot and left
their barn of fertility.
The women of the city no longer speak of love
with their husbands.
At night they do not make love.
They are no longer naked before them,
revealing intimate treasures.

Words are fast now, fast words:
Words: Deny the violent gods.
Words: Leap through the fire of your soul.
Words: Conquest kills passion.

Words are fast now—
fly from river to sky, continent to ocean, parent to child,
page to heart. In an instant, the entire world can change
its mind. Everything is possible, planets converge,
populations emerge, change, revolt, but it doesn't do any good—

We worship violent gods.
Enheduanna wrote on stone.
That is what she said.
She said we worship violent gods.

SB

The Women of Afghanistan

Maryam Azimi sent me a book in Pashtun
and Norwegian —

We need to know what it says.

We need the poems of this woman who lived with two
small children in a church in Oslo until Norway granted her
immunity from extradition so she could live with her sister —
safe in a humane country away from the Taliban.

I met her on Midsummer night.
There was a huge bonfire on the edge
of an island at the top of the world.

Women from every country —
activists, teachers, civil servants, government workers —
had come to a conference in Tromso, Norway,
400 miles above the Arctic Circle.

Slant golden light threaded us together as we talked
of children and family, the cold water, how clear it was —
Permafrost buried under ground felt like peat moss.

I met her sister first, Farida.
She was looking for shells to take back to her children.
So was I. I said I was a poet. She said they were looking
for the American poet.

I said when people at home want to find me they go to the water.
It felt like I was talking to an old friend.

Later Maryam said feminism was irrelevant, or would be until
the Taliban was gone. She said nothing else was so important.
She said we couldn't know.

I am thinking about Maryam and Farida.
I am thinking about the women of Afganistan and their children.

SB

Children of the Camp

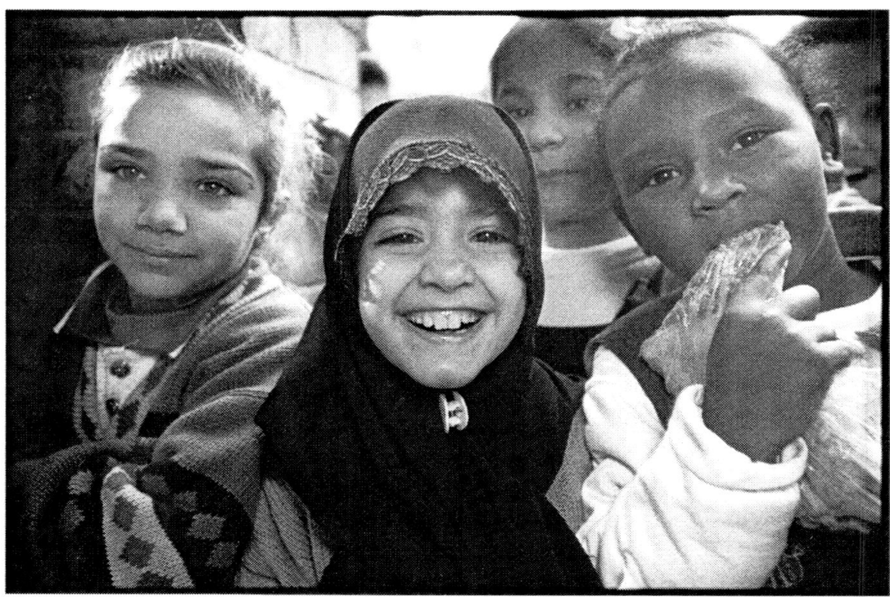

I disliked the western TV crews who came to the refugee camp. They always wanted to film the children with the bare feet, the runny noses and the dirty clothes. They could never see beyond the poverty. Their cameras could never depict the beauty that lay beyond the filth. They never sought to capture clean children on camera. Somehow, the image of cleanliness just didn't fit with the image that they wanted to portray.

The children I knew in the camp were so much different than the images depicted of them on western TV. Maram, for instance, loved to groom herself. Even at the age of 6, she would spend hours in front of the mirror, tending to her brown silky hair. Her clothes were always immaculately clean and she raced to change her blouse or pants if they ever got soiled. She was so confident and sure of herself. When her mother wasn't paying attention, Maram would sneak into her parents' bedroom and spray some perfume on herself. Then everyone would know because she would fill the house with the smell of her perfume.

Mawal was a straight A student. She was always clean and tidy, but she didn't care much for clothes. She loved reading and drawing and was exceptionally good at math. She always seemed so serious for her age. She was always polite and soft spoken, unlike her sister Rou'a. Two years younger than Mawal, Rou'a was very beautiful, with dark soft hair, two dimples and a captivating smile. Rou'a loved wearing colorful bracelets, necklaces and earnings. She was a straight A student too, but she was good at school without making much of an effort. She was very talkative in class and was always getting in trouble for talking too much. She was quite a show off.

Ala' tried to act older than his age. When his father was at work, he would play, or try to play, the role of the man of the house. He was only 5 and his two sisters, Kholoud and Sanabel, were a few years older, but he still tried to play boss. He was a very generous boy, always insisting that guests have more food than they can possibly manage to eat. He always insisted on taking a plate of hot food to his grandmother who lived with his aunt and uncle a few houses away. He was very protective of his mother and ran errands for her all the time. He wouldn't let his sisters go out in the dark unless he accompanied them. He was a chubby boy with blond hair and very fair skin.

I left so many wonderful children behind in Dheisheh refugee camp in Bethlehem. Their lives are controlled by Israel's occupation, yet the only interest that western TV crews have in them is to film their poverty.

Too bad they don't take the time to film Rana when she's dancing, or Zuzu when he's playing soccer, or Sanabel when she's singing, or Kholoud when she's screaming as the bombs start to fall.

(photograph previous page)

Smiling Girl

Dijla School for Girls, Baghdad, 1998.

Open to children of all religions, schools like this private Catholic girls school help fill the gap in education left by the Gulf War. Iraqui culture is tolerant of racial and religious diversity. Catholic aid provides textbooks and other school supplies that public schools often lack. Prior to the Gulf War, due to a nationwide initiative, literacy rates of girls and women were nearly equal to that of men and boys. Education was free through post graduate work. There was universal medical care and there were no homeless people.

MH, AP

Stand Down

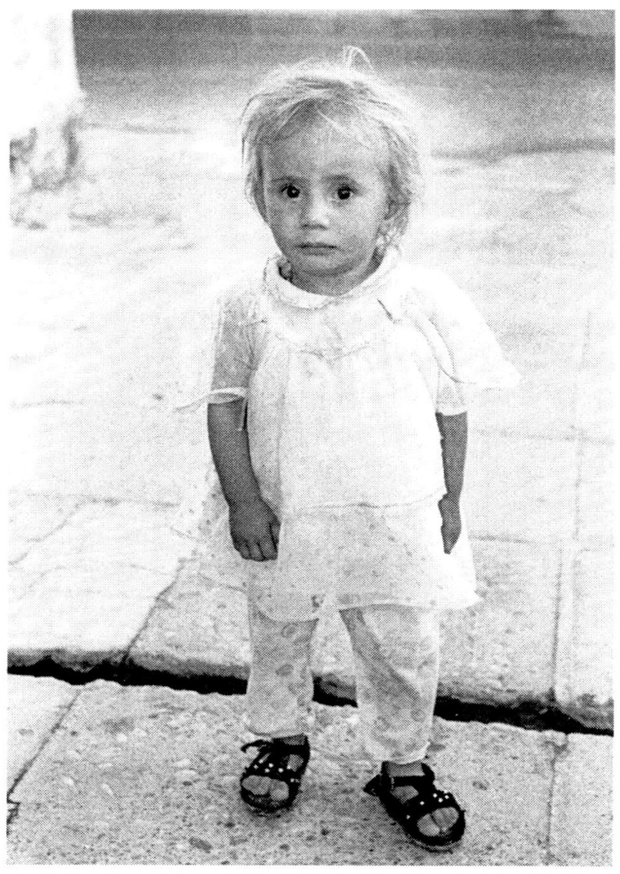

Who would argue that 911 was not an atrocity?
Or that Al Qaeda believes its cause is just?
Rhetoric pours out of FOX News Network —
a rant of *WARWARWARWARWARWARWARWAR*
and rhetoric pours out of *AL Qaeda* —
JIHADJIHADJIHADJIHADJIHADJIHADJIHAD
turbans, no turbans, beards, no beards, women's bare
faces, no women allowed.
Each truth is a mask, and everything we know
about the universe is another mask.
Babble faces rant —-
the other is so odious it must be exterminated.

The tower crumbles.

The world could have a change of heart, now.

Who says to himself, herself —
I am an idiotic, selfish, arrogant, narrow-minded, ignorant,
greedy, immoral, intolerant, power-hungry, evil coward
willing to drive humankind to extinction to impose my will on someone else?

America has been attacked and will strike back.
The attack was Al Qaeda striking back for things that happened
a thousand years ago, at the end of WWII, and next week.

An international forum exists, why not use it?
The United Nations, a World Treaty Against Terrorism,
a World Court could devolve these cycles of retaliation.

I am a poet, a woman, a parent of twin boys.
I've learned to stand down even when I'm right
because relationships are more important
than power, because power *to be* is more
important than power *over*.

I am a pacifist who cringes when the peace movement
uses the same rhetoric Al Qaeda uses to justify flying
commercial airplanes into the World Trade Center.
State imposed terror, suicide bombers —
this behavior must stop.

The world needs a peace movement with peace in it,
a dose of the nurturing wisdom of the woman.
We all need to stand down.

(photograph previous page)
Kurdish Child
City of Olives, 2000, near St. Matthews.
Child on the streets of City of Olives, a small Kurdish village north of Mosul.
SB, AP

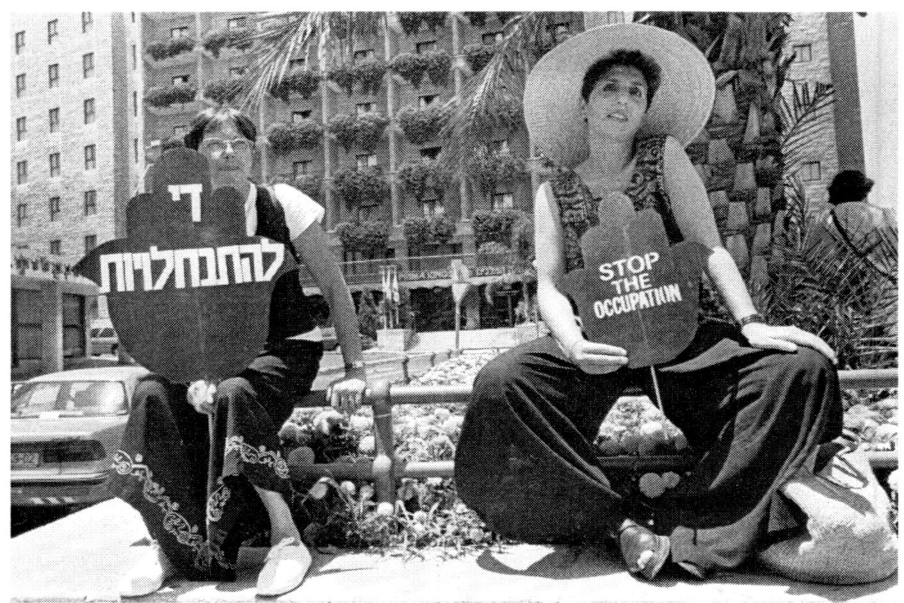

Press Your Face Against the Sky

I climb out of the creek and press my face against the sky,
stretch out on limestone warmer than the air. Light
drops points of heat into my pores.
Small drops of water linger
just a moment.

On sunny days it's warmer next to the creek than uphill,
in traffic, where the wind blows, where a human
appetite for power pushes us
to war after war.

On cold days I spread papers in the sun room where light
pours through long panes of glass until my work
space is static with dry heat. Cats wait
for me on a table splashed
with light.

I need juice —
for my computers, heat, air conditioning, don't care to wash
my clothes along the river's edge.

I like to plug things into power outlets.
Energy isn't bad. I like cars too,
the speed and convenience of them.
My life is fast, and so am I.

Today I stood with the Women in Black in front of the Capitol.
There was a slight chill in the breeze, but sunlight quickly
soaked through my dark clothing,
warming arms and back,
turning my long hair into a blanket.

We stood in front of the capitol because we want the world
to turn away from war. We want America to think
differently, act differently.

My father and grandfather were oil men whose business was
to make energy available to a society ravenous for it.
And we've grown hungrier still, so hungry that
two civilizations careen to a line drawn in
the sand, on top of oil.

911 has pushed the world to a recession.
Business responds with massive layoffs and we spin further
down into depression —

We need a million jobs —
about what it would take to change gears from carbon to light.
Invention waits for the right moment.

Press your face against the sky.

(photograph facing page) **Women in Black.** *These members of Bat Shalom, an Israeli women's peace organization nominated for the 2001 Nobel Prize for Peace, maintain a Women in Black vigil in West Jerusalem. There are peace movements in Israel and in Palestine. The Rapprochement Center does nonviolent resistance training. There are Israeli soldiers who have gone to prison rather than serve in the occupied territories. There is a Israeli group called Yesh Gvul composed of active military, retired military and conscientious objectors who maintain there can be no peace until the occupation of Palestine is over.*

SB, AP

Fly Naked

I was scheduled to fly to San Francisco a week after 911 and didn't go because I wanted to see what the Federal Aeronautic Administration would do to make flying safe. It was a mistake. I'm not comforted by the clips they show on television — air marshals tackling men wearing black hoods, and around this strange behavior a bunch of crash test dummies strapped at random angles into airplane seats. Something is wrong with the way these people think. At a meeting the other night Joyce said the answer is for everyone to fly naked. Pam said we have become a militia ready to go into action, like the one that formed on the flight that crashed in Pennsylvania. The problem is I don't really want to die in flight, plus I get cold. Maybe flight attendants could pass out extra blankets. Women may be the best defense against fundamentalist religious terrorists who can't look at us in public. A well aimed, blood soaked tampon would horrify them, shatter the ritual of gleaming clean male bodies acting in a sacred space. If terrorist camps had to invent drills for such a contingency, that alone might shut them down. Perhaps we need self-defense classes, counter terrorist brainstorming exercises instead of suitcases full of clothing or lap top computers. Any teenager knows how to terrorize adults. They could help with this. Rap lyrics on the intercom might do it. I'm just starting to invent outrageous ways to respond to outrage. What about stun gas in the cabin and a sealed off cockpit, (a lovely word) with doors set to fry anyone who touched them during a hijacking? Pilots say they can fly upside down — or bounce the plane so severely no one could remain composed, or depressurize the cabin — sort of hard on Grandfather, or a new baby, or someone trying to finish a spreadsheet, or memorize fish diseases, but it could save lives. If we can keep guns and bombs off airplanes, we can prevent them from being used for mass destruction. It might be worth screening baggage or paying workers a living wage to do that. I got an email today saying Al Qaeda terrorists should be kidnapped, given sex change operations and sent back to live as women under the Taliban. It makes me angry that someone could use my next trip to see Mother to blow up thousands of people. They would have to kill me. The thing is, I take airplanes for less drastic purpose — most of the time. The meaning of flying has just jumped scale — it might be wise to blow off the crash test dummy drill, get creative.

SB

Ode to Kansas

It begins — 911 retaliation, and we wonder when it will rain fire again as human beings curve their faces down, duck for cover. Anywhere at random the world deflates, a thousand punctures, blood pours out, poison seeps in. Ay! My country is bombing poor people again. Daytime is for airlifting supplies to refugees. Nights are for bombing military targets with smart bombs. There is nothing smart about dropping explosions out of airplanes onto human beings. In most parts of the world people think we deserved the WTC attack! They hate us. Ay! Because we're powerful? Because we are pirates? I was born in 1945. America had just saved the world from fascism. In my lifetime we've parleyed that to almost universal animosity. I've been to Kansas. It is beautiful there. People live and work and hold their children close. The sky is filling up with screams. Mountain wind and sand blow through ridges in the foothills of the Hindu Kush as refugee camps in Afghanistan fill up with people who are afraid we are going to drop nuclear bombs on them. I oppose that. I also know my country will not allow anyone else to win. I live in the most powerful nation ever invented. But power means the wrong thing, means we can take anything we want. Who would choose that kind of power? It doesn't work. It pisses people off. Remember S.A.N.E. — the Society Against Nuclear Explosions? I want power to live in freedom, power to love. My country trained the millionaire who made human bodies and fire rain from the sky in New York City. That was an obscene error — like inventing a nuclear bomb and aiming it at yourself. We have never been so vulnerable. It is less that I am afraid, though I jump at the sound of sirens. It is not that I am afraid. I've spent my life trying to avert violence. I dreamed a red and yellow airplane fell out of the sky in Los Angeles. Yesterday the water looked so intensely beautiful it seemed about to shatter. It is less that I am afraid, more that I see how vulnerable we are — the children, Kansas, Mother. In the absence of International Law, in a world where opportunists pillage at will, my country has gathered a posse to go after a stealth corporation of terrorists who are smart and rich and sick with vengeance, who are as likely to be in Kansas as someplace bombs can reach them in Afghanistan. It has begun. Our shining blue planet drifts to violent polarity. We could lose Kansas.

SB

Strange

The FBI says to be vigilant.
There are credible warnings of more terrorist attacks —

Are we to become like Hitler youth —
spy on our parents, friends, spy on anyone who looks
strange?

What's up with your hat?
Are you different?

Look for anything strange, *they tell us*.

Everything looks strange to me —
but nothing so suspicious as this president who says
to watch out for terrorists just now —

To divert our attention from essential freedoms
he has restricted?
or atrocities the bombing campaign enacts?

Has he drained our Social Security accounts to pay for this?
Eight lawmakers may be briefed. Newscasts may not play
tapes made by the enemy containing coded messages —

Are we being protected from coded messages,
or from the enemy's charisma?

Is it treason to ask?

The F.BI says to be on high alert.
The enemy is hiding among us taking aim—

Mary Ellen took her morning walk a little late this morning.
Amanda has the flu. This looks bad.

The dog just cocked one ear.

An airplane is whistling overhead.

Any moment it will rain fire on someone's home.
Airline executives will say the tail fin of an airplane broke off
for no reason. Poison is seeping into the air.

Don't open mail.

Alternative news sites are disappearing from the internet.
People who watch the School of Americas
where we train terrorists are detained at the border.

The president says to go to an amusement park.

Like small children, we are diverted from
what we don't need to know, from what the government
can do, is doing, will do in our name, without our permission —
much in the same way it came into power —
a soft-shoe accompanied by the Supremes.

Is this not strange?

SB

(photograph page 26)
Flame, Baghdad, 2000. On the banks of the Tigris River.

(photograph page 27)
Embrace, Lake Travis, Austin, TX. *I went out to Hippie Hollow, a popular swimming hole, for a story in the* **Austin Sun** *in the mid seventies about nude bathing.*

Flame

The world
rips us raw
before
our souls
are strong
enough
to imagine
peace.

Spirit
flares
as long as
possible.
We
do our
best.

There
are
instants
when
community
gathers
into
circles
of
soft
candle
light.

There
are
instants
when
we are safe
enough
to

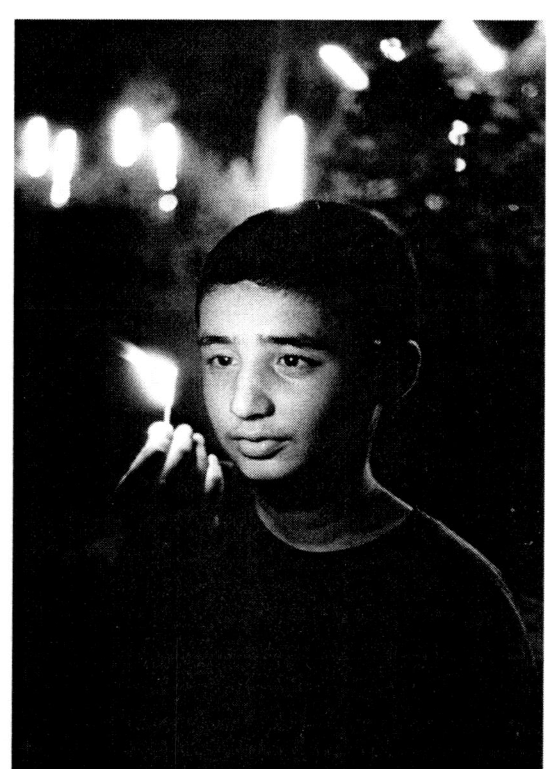

know
wonder.

I have
just
picked
seven
pungent
sprigs
of
rosemary.

My
country
is
dropping
bombs
on
human
beings.

There
is not
light
enough
to
hold
back
the
fierce
ache
of war,
the
abject
failure
of it.

Or is
there?

SB, AP

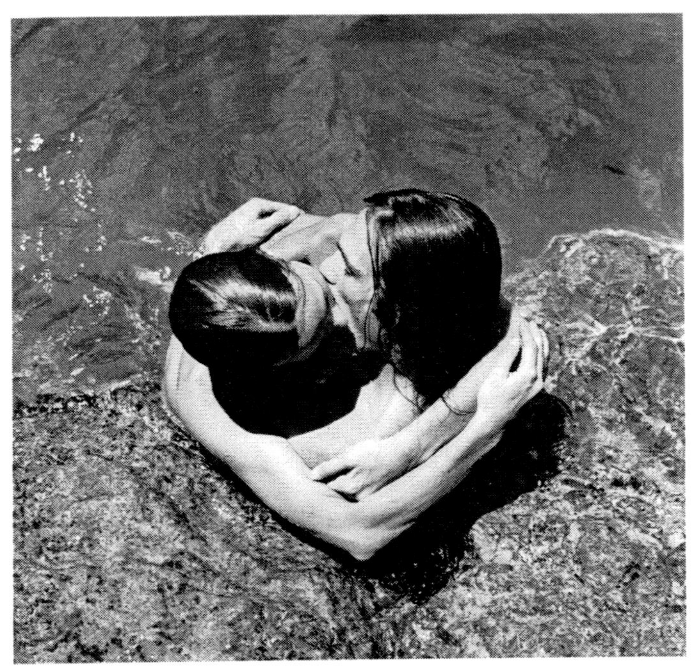

Embrace

Sometimes we rise
out of emerald
spring water
mouths pressed together,
arms knotted
around each other,
souls threaded
through each other
as if we
actually were
integral
parts of a great
living planet
swirling
always swirling,
like lovers
whose toes
and skin and mouths
and beings
pressed together
match exactly
the contour
of the Earth
we spring from
and are.

SB, AP

The Open Jar

I am sitting naked on the floor.
My soul rests exposed in an open jar next to me.
A jigsaw puzzle with a million faces is scattered by my feet.
A cigarette burns between my lips.
I am alive.

A stranger comes and holds me by the shoulders.
The music abruptly stops.
A hot muggy cloak of air seeps through the window
and wraps the room in silence.

A door slams.
My hand unconsciously knocks the open jar.
I watch my soul rapidly spill on the carpet.
It gathers in a puddle and awaits me.
I scoop it up and gently drip it on my warm belly.

A windchime rattles outside.
The music starts again.
Small pebbles of perspiration drip down
my neck and onto my small breasts.
My nipples harden and a moan of desire
escapes from my parted lips.
I am alive.

MH

The Sky Falls In Silence

In the last twenty years the number of songbirds
migrating between North and Central America
has decreased by 80%.

National Geographic, *1993*

And all I wanted was art, but I have
learned the marketplace as if it were
a song itself, a score of people listening
for hope in a century of despair.

And I have learned the names of intrigue,
have watched power plays, have played,
and won and lost, and lost the words
themselves. And the songbirds have gone.

And I have seen the error of our time.
And it is arrogance entrenched at every
intersection in the net of life—
infinitely glittering with lies.

And all the words are lies.
Philanthropy *means buying votes.*
Contributions *are hard bribes.*
Extortion *is legal if you're a judge.*

Greenbelts *are freeway medians.*
Water Quality *means sewage in the river.*
Casualty *means someone is dead.*
A Conflict *is a war that doesn't exist.*

Words that are lies cannot fashion truth.
This song is a dirge, the water is dying.
The song birds are dying, our brain cells
are twisted. And the sky falls in silence.

SB

Ay!

I tossed a red rose
on the water today,
two leaves broke away almost
immediately,
delicate on green water.

Crisp
with cold energy
I moved through water
that seemed intensely fragile
to me.

A terrorist could poison the water.

Someone who could
fly commercial airplanes
into the World Trade
Center could think of that.

Ay!
Ay!

The rose floated
downstream today.

I quickly lost
sight of it.

SB

Digging Out

My own digging out is minor — laundry and junk that accumulated while we were glued to the television, mouths stuck open in horrific awe, followed by days glued to the internet engaged in a great debate — *What shall we do about what we seem to be doing? About what we have done?* This followed by days of grief, tears and more tears and meetings, rallies and more meetings. So today, eleven days after 911, as I sweep and clear out the debris of an American family, I think it is good to be in my own skin, in my home, engaging friends and loved ones who are mostly fine. I light candles for the people clearing away unspeakable debris at ground zero in New York — a seven story high mass grave for thousands of people — body parts, birds with charred wings. I wake up in the night thinking of airplanes flying into the World Trade Center, cannot go back to sleep. My own anxieties are small triggers that open me to the greater fear, the greater loss, the greater grief, *America the Beautiful, Ay! Ay!* I write letters to everyone — senators, congress people, friends, do laundry, engage in the great debate. The war machine ratchets up. Our government sends ships to defeat a landlocked country fraught with famine and patriarchal oppression. Ay! It's like turning off a light with a jack hammer. I saw a film of Afghan street life — women in long robes and masks, blue Burkas — lumps of form holding wide-eyed children with naked faces. Anything could be hidden beneath these walking tents — heroine, guns, Al Qaeda operatives. I hang up lingerie, fold towels, thankful to be safe. How long will we be safe? I sweep dog hair out from under the computer table, talk to my sister on the telephone, make tacos, negotiate a new job. It's Saturday in America. The stuff of daily life has a new pallor, a sweet necessity to it. We call each other *dearest*, sign notes with words that say the love we used to hide, ignore, gloss over. Poets think up eloquent ways to curb the maniac. I sweep. I sweep, thankful for the simple rhythm of it, thankful for the small debris of life, tell everyone — *send a peace petition, hug a fireman, love somebody, write a letter, think of something we can do that's not mass murder.* America isn't finished being true, we've hardly begun.

SB

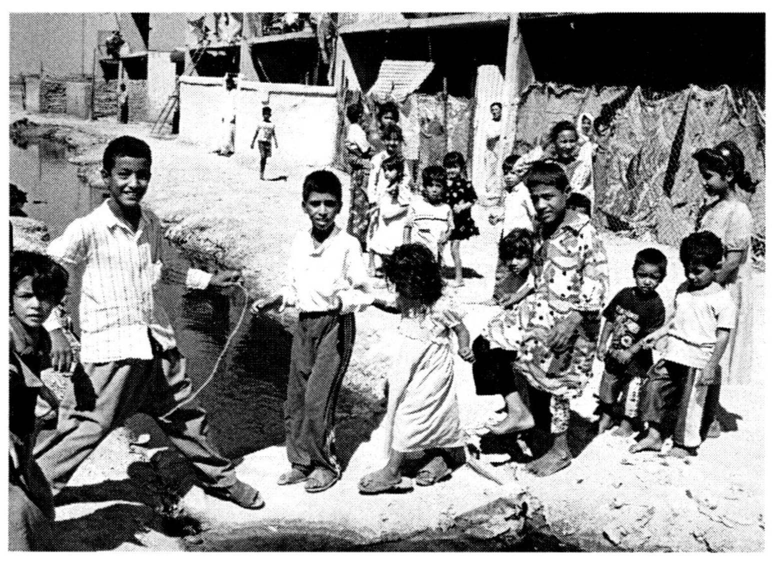

Who Will Protect the Children of 'Aida Refugee Camp?

Bethlehem — Ali Jawariesh looked so young and innocent as his lifeless body, covered with a gleaming Palestinian flag, lay on the stretcher waiting to be taken for burial. Yet his face, still and peaceful, did not seem to be that of a seven-year-old first-grader. His eyelids were puffy, the hair at the front of his head had been shaved, and an ugly, scar protruded across his forehead. This is where the bullet of an Israeli army sniper landed when Ali was shot in 'Aida Refugee Camp on November 11. The rubber-coated metal bullet was fired from a range of 15 meters, leaving Ali braindead for five days before he was officially declared dead on November 15. Ironically, the announcement of his death came as Palestinians were celebrating the anniversary of their declaration of independence.

At his funeral on November 16, Ali's young classmates looked stricken with grief as they carried a placard reading "students of the Elementary first grade" and wept in silence. Ali was a bright, quiet student, and popular in class. Less than an hour before he was shot, he returned home from school with his report card in hand. He had received a grade point average of all A's, and after showing it to his parents, he rushed out of the house. Ali was eager to show his grades to an aunt who lives nearby.

Shortly thereafter, a distraught Imad Hanash, a car mechanic who runs a car repair shop nearby, was rushing Ali to the hospital in his car. "I found Ali's blood and small pieces of his brain in the back seat of the car," says Hanash. "Cleaning up the mess was one of the hardest things I ever had to do. I'll never get over it." Hanash believes that Ali was shot with a live, and not a rubber-coated metal, bullet. "As I carried him in my arms, I could see the long bullet sticking a few centimeters out of his head," says Hanash. "A metal bullet is round and would not have been visible."

According to eyewitnesses, Ali was standing with a group of stone-throwing children in Zone A (under Palestinian control) of 'Aida Refugee Camp, when an Israeli soldier at Rachel's Tomb — in Zone C (under Israeli control), 60 meters away — came down the hill and shot him. The situation at the Tomb had been tense for two days. Hundreds of Israeli religious fanatics were celebrating the official opening of the Tomb, and dancing crazily in the street under the protection of heavily armed Israeli soldiers. The two-day celebrations came after the Israeli authorities completed construction of a stone wall around the Tomb, as well as a stone watchtower.

"An Israeli soldier approached me earlier that morning and ordered me to disperse a group of stone-throwing children," explains Hanash. "He told me that there were too many Israelis around and he did not want to risk their lives. I replied that the children were too young to pose a threat and that they would go away by themselves." When the soldier persisted, Hanash suggested that he, the soldier, call the District Coordination Office (DCO) — the joint Israeli-Palestinian military coordination outfit — who could send out a Palestinian army patrol to peacefully disperse the children. The soldier refused and for the remainder of the day, he kept harassing Hanash. At 2 p.m., the soldier told Hanash he had until 4 p.m. to disperse the boys.

"He threatened me and told me that after 4 p.m. he would not be responsible for what happens." It was at 4 p.m. that Israeli defense minister Yitzhak Mordechai was expected to arrive at Rachel's Tomb to participate in the celebrations. Shortly after Mordechai's arrival, Ali was shot and, according to Palestinian press reports, it is widely believed that it was one of the minister's guards who fired at Ali.

Ahmed Salah, a mechanic at Hanash's shop who witnessed the shooting, says that Israeli soldiers had caught several young boys earlier that day. "They beat them up and let them go," he says. "The children later set fire to a tire, and I was ordered at gunpoint to put out the fire. But too many stones were flying in the air, and I could not get near." Salah says that a few minutes before Ali Jawariesh was shot, five Israeli soldiers came running down the road after a group of young kids. "One of the soldiers grabbed a boy, threw him on the ground and placed his boot over the boy's neck. The soldier then leaned down on his other knee, aimed his sniper gun, and fired at Ali's head.

"He fired to kill," says Ahmed Jawariesh, Ali's uncle. "Ali was only seven for God's sake! The soldier could have aimed at his legs if he had meant to injure him rather than kill him." Eyewitnesses at the scene say that right after Ali was shot, the soldiers arrested three refugee children, ages 12, 11 and 10. "They put them in the jeep and took them to Etzion [an Israeli military camp near Hebron], where they beat the living daylights out of them," says Sheik Abu Nasser, the father of one of the children. "At midnight, the jeep dropped the boys off at the Bethlehem checkpoint and ordered them to walk home." Abu Nasser's son, Tha'er, 12, suffered from severe pain in his stomach, back, legs and arms from the beating. "He came home limping from the pain in his leg."

Hanash and several camp residents told Palestine Report that skirmishes between young refugee children under the age of 12 and Israeli soldiers stationed at Rachel's Tomb is a daily occurrence. "It is a worrying situation," says Hanash. "The Israelis who usually come to pray at Rachel's Tomb are fanatics and we always worry that one of them might randomly open fire at the children." Area residents fear a repeat of the massacre by Israeli settler Baruch Goldstein, who opened fire at Muslim worshipers, including children, in Hebron in early 1994.

"There ought to be a permanent Palestinian military point between the camp and Rachel's Tomb to protect the children," says one camp resident. "Where is the security coordination between the Israelis and the Palestinians? If the Israelis were holding these celebrations, with so many religious fanatics present, why wasn't there a reinforcement of Palestinian forces, to prevent the children from approaching the Tomb?" Camp residents further complain that Israeli undercover units repeatedly enter the camp, indicating that undercover units were in 'Aida just one month ago. As one resident puts it, "the location of 'Aida is very sensitive, and this is why we need permanent Palestinian army points at the borders of the camp."

Meanwhile, Ali's father, Mohammed Jawariesh, looked dazed and numb from the grief and lack of sleep as he received the hundreds of mourners and answered questions from the local and foreign press. The press was mostly interested in knowing what prompted him to donate his son's organs — an unprecedented decision by the parent of a martyr and considered somewhat taboo in a Muslim society which still frowns upon organ donations and autopsies. The press also wanted to confirm the news that Mohammed had donated the organs to needy recipients, whether Arabs or Jews.

"The organ donation bothers the Israelis," says Khaled, a family friend. "They kill the boy and the father turns around, before the entire world, and donates his son's organs to people who could possibly be Jewish. It is embarrassing to the Israelis." Perhaps it is the embarrassment which prompted the Israeli Minister of Health and the Minister of Defense to call Ali's father to extend their condolences. "Mohammed spoke to them briefly, saying he was in no shape to talk, and hung up," says Ahmed Jawariesh. "In one phone call, he was asked to go meet with some high-level military person on November 17, who wanted to apologize to him. When Mohammed refused, they tried to urge him by saying that they had a gift for him but we have no idea what they meant by that."

The donation of Ali's organs was the talk of the week in Bethlehem. Some people considered the father's decision courageous, others thought it was against the teachings of Islamic religion, but all followed the news to learn the identity of the organ recipients who, as it turned out, were all Israeli Arabs.

Meanwhile, little attention was paid to the serious question raised by Ali's untimely death: Who will protect the children of 'Aida from further Israeli attacks?

Palestine Report, 21 November 1997.

(photograph page 36)

Kids Crossing Ditch

Basra, 1998.

Children cross open sewer outside of unfinished housing project. This complex is home to 8,000 internally displaced Iraqi's.

MH

Do Not Forget in Peace Times

"A nation which is formed by fraud or blood is condemned to repeat that pattern until it is overcome by a greater, more violent or more fraudulent power."
Jean Saint De Crevecoeur

Do not forget in peace times to teach the children
about violence, how it swirls out of the center of everyone,
how each must own their own quotient of it,
must order the chaos of it in their private soul.
Do not forget in peace times to teach the children, that
war seeds war, comes from unhealed fights whose blood raw
wounds callous over, hard and dull, doctrinaire—
like smooth silver film, a celluloid tablet of the world.
Do not forget in peace times to teach the children
how the wounded ones project their pain onto the world
at Auschwitz, or Salem, finding witches or Jews, or saints
or Iranians, or Africans, or anyone, maybe you.
Do not forget in peace times to teach the children
each act of violence seeds the next.

(Photograph facing page) **Eternal Presence**, 1999. A man in the Zapista autonomous community of Polho.

SB

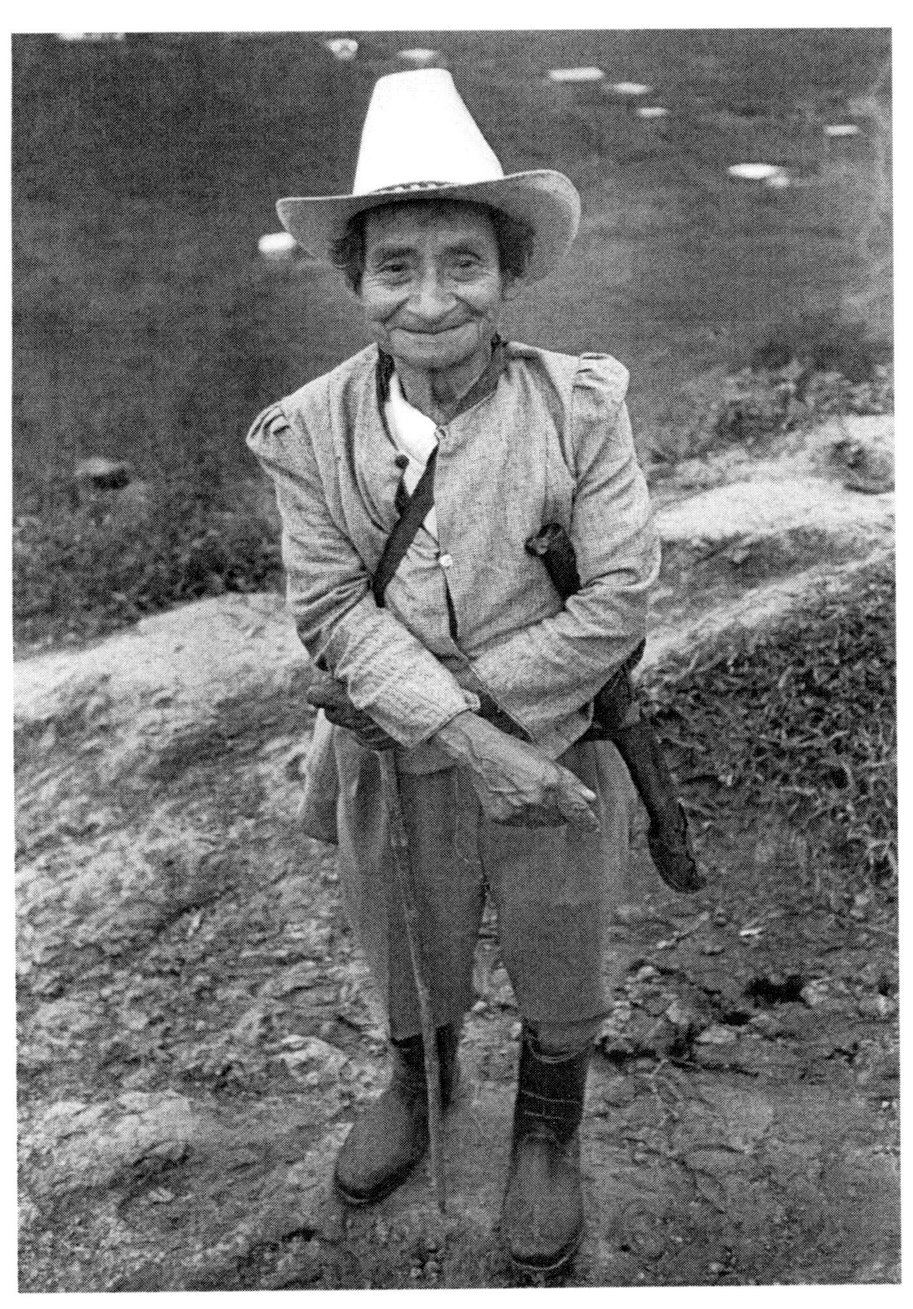

I am always and forever of this place.

AP

The German Question

I always wondered how they could have allowed it to occur.
Were they intrinsically evil or blind, or duped by a dialectic,
an idea, religion, provinciality?

I always thought it couldn't happen here because it was too
horrific, because it is obviously wrong to kill vast numbers
of innocent people, or any.

But now we are doing exactly that and because I remember
the German question, the killing of 18,000,000 witches in Europe,
a million people in Rwanda and Sierra Leone,
a million and a half people in Iraq —
I know what is happening, I remember the German question.

I thought perhaps they were busy, doing chores, sweeping the street,
taking care of their children, cooking supper, running businesses?

But their Jewish neighbors were being herded into ghettos
around the corner, across the tracks. There was gunfire, Krystal Nacht,
businesses were mysteriously closed, taken over by someone else,
ash floating down the street, gathering on window sills,
burning flesh on feather dusters, public executions.

So the question is how do we grow blind to what is happening
before our faces, on television, over the fence,
in the immediate vicinity, here and now.
How many maimed children does one have to see?

And then the question becomes —
seeing it, how do we avert a humanitarian crises
of unimaginable proportion — now!
babies and mothers dying in open tents in harsh winter
in the high plainsof the Hindu Kush—

The German question —
since I could think I wondered how it could possibly have occurred.

SB

Black Cross

American F-117A Stealth Nighthawk Fighters fly under radar and maneuver so quickly they are considered invisible.
Robert Fisk, British journalist, **The Independent**, March, 1998.

It lit up all of Europe as it fell, the old woman said,
Milicia Lalosevic, a simple village woman of Budjanovic,
whose children and neighbors dance on the wings
of an American Stealth jet, villagers spinning in dance,
villagers ripping black metal from the fuselage, relics for the church—
a toothless man winking, *They make paint that's invisible.*

These are the words of Robert Fisk.
These are the words of Milicia Lalosevic,
a simple village woman.

Revelers macabre in thick morning fog, thrust three Serbian fingers
at the sky, shout *Victory!*

An invisible black cross in the sky shot down by Serbian villagers
is unreported in the American press.

We are combating genocide, say the joint chiefs of state.

II
There are international laws against genocide but no way
to enforce them, no way to try *para-military* war criminals —
100,000 Rwandans detained in detention camps for mass murder.
What court can hear so much evidence? Who can listen to such horror?

III
Ethnic Cleansing—
Serbs arrive at dawn, force Albanians out of their homes,
execute the leaders, load people who aren't dead onto trucks, trains,
ship them to the border, no papers, no possessions,
burn their homes, declare a city *cleansed—*

Continued

At the border there are too many women and children.
Where did the men go?

A city scrubbed clean in this way can be resettled by cousins of villagers
in Budjanovic, who dance on the wing of an American Stealth jet,
people who can be convinced to commit mass murder, or tolerate it,
people who work in factories making American Stealth jets,
people who throng to a rock concert in Belgrade undaunted by bombs.

IV.

Help us, say the Albanian women.
They have taken our men to the military targets.

In the newspaper there is a photograph of concert-goers
holding babies on their shoulders. They have painted targets
on their children's caps!

People throw heads back and shout at the sky, *Hit me! Hit me!*
rock music blaring as the black cross which is invisible,
traces a fast shadow scouring the Earth, becomes a death machine,
makes Serbs love Milosovic who last week hated him —
three Serbian fingers punching Sky.

The rock star is married to Arkan —
an indicted war criminal, called the Tiger, who designed ethnic cleansing.
In her music videos she makes love to a Tiger cub, is his third wife.
They have two lovely children.

V

In the village of Budjanovic, an old priest holds up a piece of scrap
metal torn from the wing of a US Stealth jet, a chunk of black
metal twisted like a crucifix.

It is the bone of a saint, god blood for communion.
It is the Shroud of Turin, a piece of the True Cross, a shard
of the military god we worship.

SB

Bethlehem Man Leads Crusade For the Environment

If Imad Atrash has his way, nobody in Palestine will smoke, no babies will use disposable diapers, and no empty plot of land will be left without forestation.

Atrash is so environmentally conscious it has even rubbed off on his three young children. When his four-year old daughter wants to call someone, usually another child, a bad name, she blurts the words "you're environmental pollution," making her father laugh with pride.

Born and raised in the predominantly Christian town of Beit Sahour, Atrash admits that his passion for nature and the environment used to make him stick out like a sore thumb. "People used to mock me when I went out with my camera to take wildlife pictures," he laughs. "They felt sorry for my father for raising such a 'weird' son."

Tossing the opinions of others to the wind, Atrash went on with his work and photographed more than 1200 species of wild plants, dozens of birds and mammals, and hundreds of nature sites in Palestine.

His hard work and persistence eventually paid off. Atrash has published many of his photos in educational texts on nature preservation and posters of his work are often seen hanging on office walls. One poster, of migratory birds against a beautiful sunset, has the words "migratory birds know no boundaries" printed on top.

"I use terms like 'nature knows no boundaries' in all my posters to make a political statement," explains Atrash. "It drives the Israelis crazy."

For the past few years, Atrash has been working as director of the Children for the Protection of Nature in Palestine (CPNP), an environmental education program begun by the Lutheran Schools in Jerusalem. The philosophy of the center is to inspire and foster a better understanding and appreciation of the natural environment through education. "Initially, we started working with five Lutheran Schools and now we work with 50 schools throughout Palestine," he says. "We supervise the environmental activities of the students and we train teachers on how to become environmental educators."

Most of the 250 volunteers who work with CPNP are schoolteachers. In addition to his work at CPNP, Atrash is also editor-in-chief of Shqae'q al-Nouma'n (Anemone Corinaria), a quarterly magazine published by the center and the Education for Awareness and Involvement program, a project established in 1985 by the Lutheran schools in cooperation with Birzeit University to modify school curricula.

But getting where he is today wasn't easy for Atrash. "After 13 years of working as a lab technician in the science department at Bethlehem University, I quit my job in 1992 and dedicated myself to nature preservation and environmental issues," he recalls, the excitement of that move still evident in his voice. "The beginnings were humble and it was not until two years later that my work was taken seriously by the public."

In 1994, Atrash and 15 other amateur Palestinian environmentalists attended a training program run by the Royal Society for the Preservation of Nature in Jordan. "When we returned to Palestine, the public seemed to finally realize that there were actually people out there interested in preserving nature and the environment," he says. "So we held seven successful training programs in the country and this is how we ended up having 250 volunteers working with us."

In addition to giving lectures all over Palestine and participating in international conferences on the preservation of the environment, Atrash is also busy setting up an Environmental Education Center at the Talita Lutheran School in Beit Jala, the first of its kind in Palestine. There are plans to open similar centers in Gaza, Jericho, Ramallah and Nablus but, as Atrash points out, everything takes time and money.

Meanwhile, the center in Beit Jala is expected to open next spring. It will include a natural history museum, a section for watching migratory birds via the Internet, environmental experiments such as recycling, and a section for developing environmental awareness in school curricula.

"The natural history museum will include nearly 1,000 preserved wildlife species, including 500 species preserved in 1917," explains Atrash. Hundreds of these species were donated by Isa Attallah, an educator from Beit Sahour, Mazen Qumsieh of Beit Sahour and the Martin Luther School in Jerusalem. "Attallah donated the entire museum of his late son, Dr. Sana Attallah, who died in a car accident in Iran in the early 1970s," Atrash explains. "Dr. Sana's museum includes hundreds of animal species that lived in Palestine and the Middle East, in addition to some species from other parts of the world."

In between his work at CPNP and the magazine, Atrash finds time to give lectures to interested groups on environmental issues. Last week, he spoke at a three-day workshop held by the Palestinian Agricultural Relief Committee in Bethlehem. His topic was the role of women in the preservation of the environment. He passionately warned his audience on the use of chemicals, such as chlorine, in house cleaning.

“I don’t understand why things that our grandmothers used as household cleaners, such as vinegar, have to be replaced with something poisonous like chlorine!”

But while Atrash has seen a groundswell of public interest in the environment, he is still less than optimistic. “Environmentally speaking, I am very depressed,” he told Palestine Report. “We have a problem with pollution, sewage, industrial zones situated in residential areas, as well as disposable diapers.” Atrash insists that disposable diapers, which take up to 100 years to degrade, are an environmental catastrophe in Palestine.

Atrash is equally gloomy about the Bethlehem 2000 Project, which hopes to attract five million tourists to the city where Christ was born. “Where are we going to get food and water from for these tourists?” he asks. “We will have to start planting our land with 10 crop cycles per year if we want enough food for all the tourists. And where will the trash and the refuse of these tourists go? The percentage of pollution in our reservoirs is already quite high, so how are we going to deal with all the extra sewage?”

Atrash is convinced that if five million tourists descend on Bethlehem in the span of five days, the local residents will pay the price. “They will be victims with no way out,” he says. “The year 2000 looks very bleak and we haven’t even come close to making any plans to deal with getting set up.”

Palestine Report, 17 October 1997.

MH

(photograph page 49)

Common Area, Coffield Unit, Texas Department of Criminal Justice, 1984,

What We Fear

When I arrived in Washington D.C. the summer of 1968,
Marshal Law had just been proclaimed. Street corners, particularly
around the Justice Department, swarmed with police officers.

The Poor People's Campaign had just arrived in horse-drawn wagons,
had come to peacefully inform the world of a vast array
of unjust conditions people of color endure in America.

Summer showers, that cooled nothing down, made D.C. streets
and sidewalks steam, turned their encampment into slick, warm mud.
D.C. was smoldering from fires that erupted after
the death of Martin Luther King.

I lived in a renovated townhouse on 9th St. S. E.,
in a black neighborhood, was threatened every time I stepped
outdoors, but small children could play on the street
until the small hours of the morning.

When I followed Jesse Jackson and the poor people around
D.C. — to schools and community centers, to potluck lunches
and street corner meetings, no one yelled at me.

I was safe, the way I'd been safe at the three-generation church
suppers Mother, Grandmother, Sister and I attended in Illinois.

I was twenty-three years old, not a freedom rider, just a young woman
trying to understand America, who had the honor of experiencing
Martin Luther King's message of peaceful resistance,
who stood a moment with the community he spoke for.

The second manifestation of military law in the nation's capital
in my lifetime occurred when a hijacked United Airlines commercial
jet was flown into the Pentagon.

I am still only one woman trying to understand the world,
and I wonder what these two incidents, one peaceful, one violent,
have in common?

SB

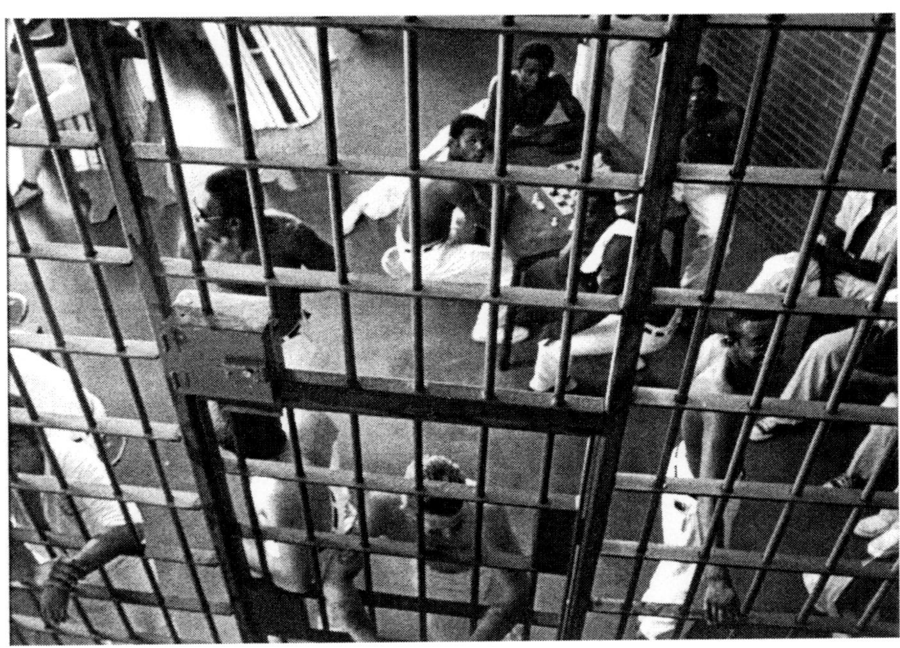

Symmetry

Where is the line
between what happens to you
and what occurs to me?

At the back gate
of Barton Springs I tell
Phillip about my
ten million
dollar rule —
that no one should
be allowed to have
any more than
ten million dollars.
That is enough.

Anything in excess of
ten million dollars
has to go back to society —
to schools, hospitals,
cultural events,
housing, social programs,
rehabilitation.

Anyone who refuses
to cooperate with the
ten million dollar rule
goes to jail.

Today jails
are full of poor people —
poor people of color.
Parents are powerless
to keep their children
out of jail, off the street,
safe from war.

Change that.

SB, AP

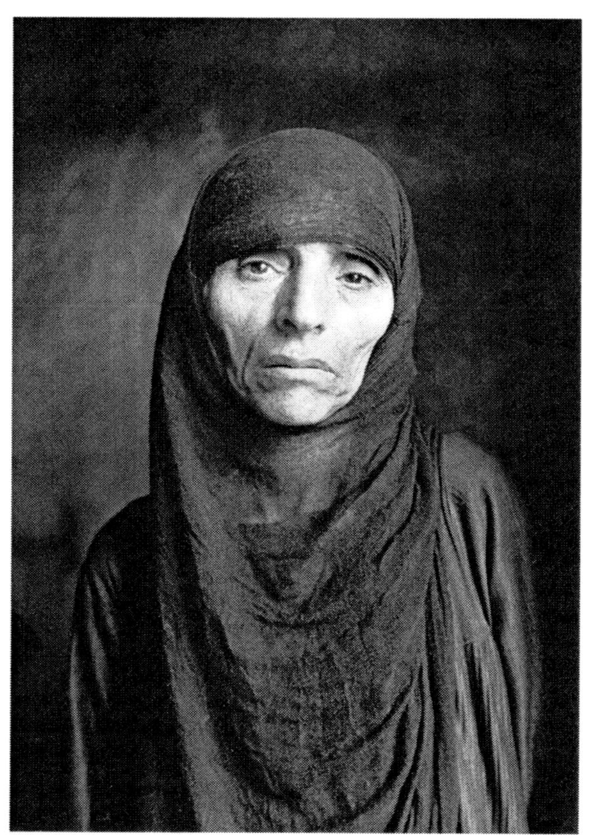

Sad Woman, taken in Basra, in an unfinished housing project for displaced people in July '98. This woman is one of 600,000 Iraqis displaced by the Gulf War. She lives in an unfinished, two story concrete structure. There is no inside plumbing. The temperature in Basra during July and August reaches 128F. This woman has very painful swollen joints, but receives no medical care. One of her sons lost his foot in the Iran/Iraq war and receives the equivalent of $5 per month.

When I took her picture she said, *This is no way for human beings to live*.

AP

To Understand

I pull your face
over my soul,
a mask —

quickly scrape
it away.

Ay!

Fisherman

He's been standing
in the surf all day
catching small
whitefish
and pompano
with a cane pole
and strong black line,
in case
a big one bites —
a redfish
or yellow jack
or sea trout.

He'd have to walk
it out
or let it go
because
he doesn't use a reel,
just his two hands
and a cigarette
to cut the line
or burn off a
hook.

The clear blue ocean
shines in his eyes.

He smells
of salt and sweat,
of fish
and smoke.

He's lean
and just a little
hungry.

Tonight he will
be a joyful
lover.

SB

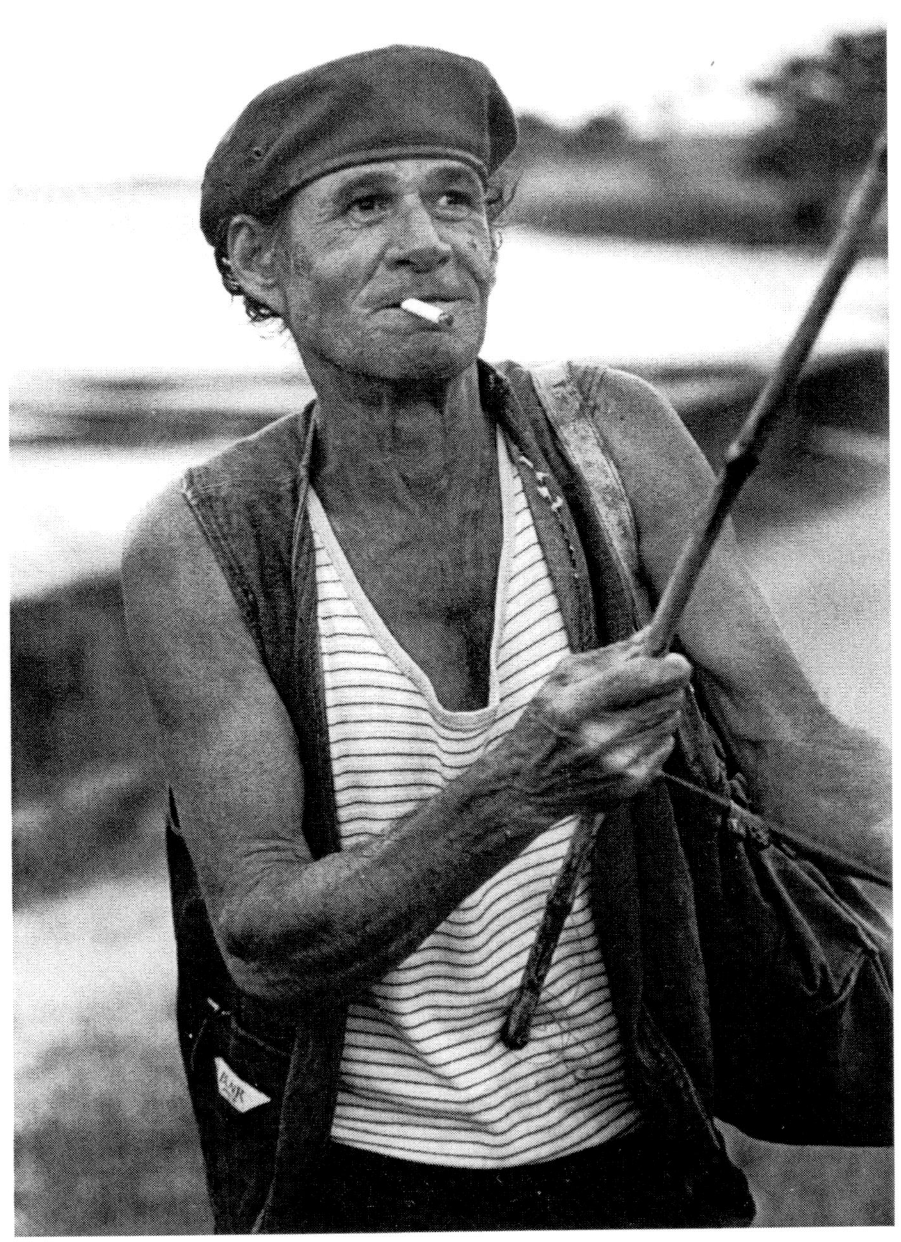

Pescadero, Cuba, 1999.
He has eudaimonia, happiness derived by being blessed with a good genius.

AP

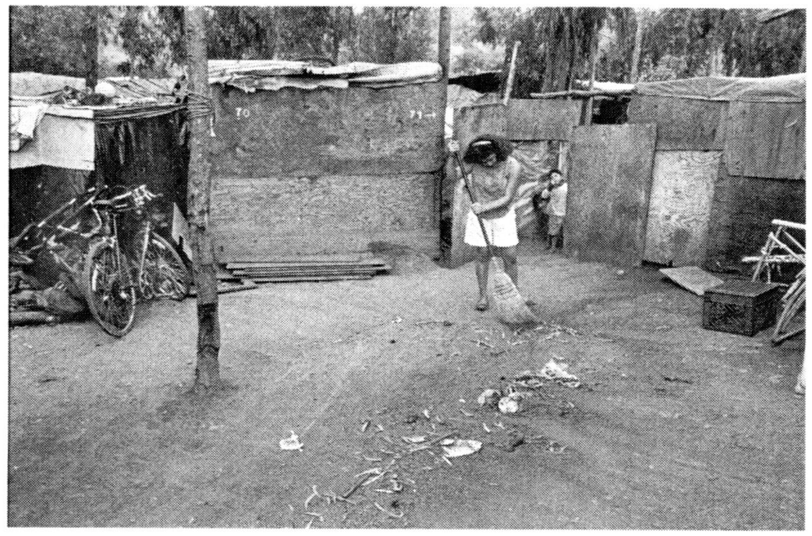

The girl sweeping the dirt is one of 45,000 farm workers in San Diego county. The agricultural product was worth 2.2 billion in 1992, when I was there. The farm and packing shed owners are not required to supply housing, so many thousands of laborers live in pieced together shelters, abandoned cars, under trees, and in holes in the ground (I have pictures of the holes with old car seats and milk crates in them for furniture). One agribusiness owner, Mr. Singh, who came from India, proposed building a motel-like structure for single men farm workers and he was bitterly opposed by the other growers. Having known misery himself, he built it in spite of their objections.

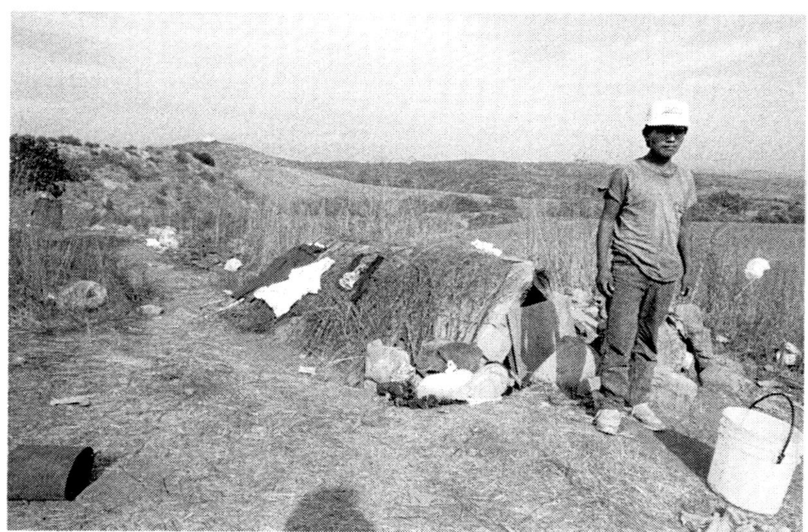

This cardboard and grass shelter is his only home. This is not an unusual situation in San Diego. The young man was complaining of heart pain. The medical worker could not find anything wrong and concluded it was stress.

AP

Campsite

No trout stream, no L.L. Bean tent with dormer flaps
and screen porch, no down bags, no campsite bathrooms,
hot showers, no Land Rovers, no long afternoon for sleeping,
no whitefish in the surf, no chaise lounge
for Mother who reads mystery novels, no carrying case
for pets too spoiled to stay home.

No water skis. No school bus. No school.
A makeshift shack to live in.
14 hour days in the fields, or in food processing plants.

No *per diem*. No travel expenses. No living wage.
Nowhere to live. Hitch to a post office. Send money back to Mexico,
Guatemala, El Salvador.

No protection from *migre* who oddly come on payday.

Rifles snap across a field!
One shot in the spine. Eight trucked back across the border.

Plywood walls, a piece of tin, blue tarps, a grave-sized hole
to live in, no health care or retirement income, supper in a plastic
bag, coyote on the hill, laundry drying in the light,
clean and sweet, like Mother said to do.

Do the math.
45,000 farm workers bring in a 2.2 billion dollar crop.

Dirt to sweep beneath an open sky,
family to tend.

SB

Mother, Washing
Chiapas, Mexico, 1999.

Near Acteal, the site of the largest recent massacre of the indigenous Mayan population. She is concerned to see the photographer and companion in a dangerous area. Political violence drives many people north away from family and home, to populate the colonias and work in maquiladoras.

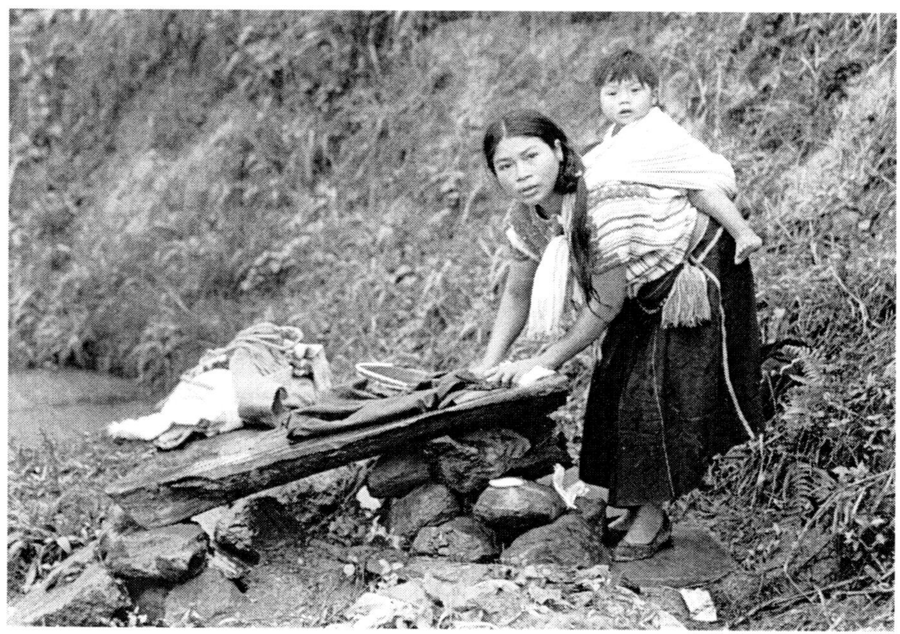

This mother must continue to do the basic work of life: growing, gathering and cooking food; spinning, weaving, sewing and washing clothes; bearing and caring for children. We notice each other in an instant of communication. She continues her work. I bring her image to others, which is my work, so that they may appreciate through her the struggle of the Mayan people, the indigenous people, of Chiapas.

AP

Indigenous

There were eleven points —
housing, land, work, food, health, education, justice,
independence, liberty, democracy and peace.

The child rides his mother like a small monkey
as she bends to the washing stone along the river
near Acteal in Chiapas.

Uphill, a man with coal black hair and lean arms
cuts wood with an axe.

They do not complain about hard work.

This Mayan woman speaks two languages,
can use a rifle and the internet, is pregnant
for the second time.

See how mother and child match the fabric of the land
exactly. It is the meaning of indigenous.

(photograph proceeding page) **Laura Bonaparte**, originator of The Mothers of the Plaza in Argentina, 1994. *SB*

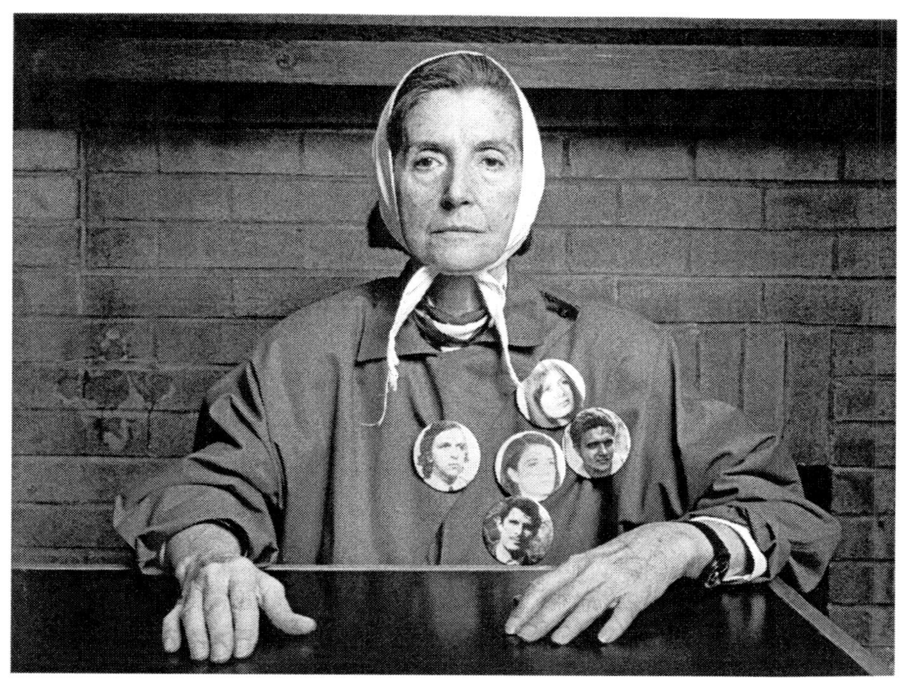

Mother of the Disappeared

Angelina
is a quiet baby, I wrap
her to my breast
with cornflower cloth
and do my work.

I am sixteen.
Miguel comes to the
center row, with water
and ripe fruit.

He takes my breath away.

Angelina holds
Maria's arm when
she takes her first step.
They are proud,
laugh together —

clap,
fall down laughing.

My girls take blue tortillas
for travelers
at the bus stop.

We find my daughters
bodies at the land fill.

I cannot say this.
I want to talk about before —

Nilo
is a crying baby,
the women say his stomach
is not finished. I hold him all
the time. He cries every minute.
Later he is the strongest one.
Girls like Nilo.
They watch his black eyes
flash. He is an officer,
like his father, when they
come to our home.

Carlos
is an easy child.
He wants to be with Miguel
more than his mother.
By that time I am
glad to have a rest.

Now I want more
time for Carlos.
He is the smartest one —
They say he will
be a priest.
He went there.

They kill Carlos
and our priest.

Miguel and Nilo are shot
in the head.
We find their bodies
alongside the wall
next to the church.
Blood turns
the flowers brown.

Now I am
Mother of the Disappeared.
Five buttons on my shirt.

One for each child,
and one for Miguel.
The Mothers make
these pictures for me.
I speak
so you will know.

These are my children
and my husband —
disappeared.

I look at your faces
and see mothers.

Those people who murder
my children are poor like me.

Why does your country
give them guns to kill my family?

SB, AP

Thoughts Written in the Sand

This country has taught me a great deal about loneliness.
Days pass by and my friends are plenty,
but silent desolation lingers on,
unshaken by the noise of daily life.

I miss hearing Arabic music blaring from small shops in
*souqs** burdened with the weight of time.
I crave the rich aroma of falafel floating from humble food
stands in neighborhoods ancient with the taste of time.
I yearn for the liveliness of the children in the refugee camps,
their dark eyes smiling despite their impoverished lives.

I find myself tired of this country,
a country that makes me feel so serious and so old;
a country I cannot call my home.

I want to stare at a flying bird.
I want to imagine I have wings and can race
the seagulls to the shore.
I want to run barefoot in the rain
and devour the smell of the life as it
rises from the wet earth.
I want to write my thoughts in the sand,
and watch a hungry wave soak them
into the tireless memory of time.

** souqs: old markets found throughout the Middle East*

MH

Quick, Before the World Gets Organized

Jump scale. Imagine you are a multinational corporation who wants to dump nuclear waste in Mexico. Trade is free, so you do it, but the Mexican government says, *No*. This is good. You keep your toxic waste and sue Mexico for 15.6 million dollars. It's called Investor-to-State Dispute Resolution. The next year you sue another government who tries to regulate toxic waste in violation of free trade — *ad infinitum* until the world gets organized. You're like the farmer whose strategy is what *not* to plant. The free market is a shell game, watch the money trail. Jump scale again. You are the most powerful nation on the earth. You've been attacked by terrorists, not by a nation state, by a bunch of pissed-off, low-tech fundamentalists who want a holy war. It is an asymmetrical attack, like David and Goliath. The UN Charter gives you the right to defend yourself from an immediate or ongoing attack. But the attack, which killed thousands of civilians and caused enormous devastation, was over in 30 minutes. A month later you initiate military action against a small country thought to harbor the enemy. You bomb cities, Red Cross centers, villages, homes and enemy encampments. Your allies in the various treaty organizations are obliged to help you defend yourself. But are you really doing that? Some say you are in violation of international law and much of the world is furious. You could have joined with all nations in the United Nations Security Council to form a world treaty to stop terrorism. You could have worked to have the thugs who attacked you tried in the World Court. Instead you form a posse of rich countries and declare war against one of the poorest countries on the planet. Nevermind last summer you were negotiating a pipeline deal with the government you are now going to annihilate. Now you have a better way to get Asian oil. You don't want a United Nations treaty against terrorism because you conduct terrorist operations in perhaps a dozen member states, plus partisan loyalties and opportunism are rampant there — not unlike the situation in your own legislature where a radical coup is using national catastrophe to squeeze huge corporate gains from the public trust — two billion dollars, for instance, to Ford Motor Company so they can go on making inefficient cars. Billions to airlines who don't screen baggage. But that's ok. You like oil dependent industry, you are an oil man. Plus your father has major financial interest in the 11th largest munitions corporation in the world. You wanted a Middle Eastern war

Continued

and have been given one on a silver platter. One thing you don't want is renewable energy. Another is peace. It's too much trouble to comply with international law, to gather viable evidence, present it to a world judicial body you don't control, easier to assassinate suspects. So that's what you do. The small country can prove to any court's satisfaction that you are dropping bombs on them. Your evidence of the guilt of small villages in the Hindu Kush which you annihilate, is non-existant. Plus your detective work is secret so you create a Military Tribunal with no jury, in which no evidence necessary, in which can sentence anybody to death. You inform the world you have the right to assassinate anyone anywhere on earth you suspect of plotting terrorism against you. You are all law and all justice. The last thing you want is for the world to get organized. International Law is an ad hoc bunch of conflicting treaties, trade agreements, international bodies and charters, no coherence and no authority that is greater than the might you wield. Power trumps ethics. And that's good. The most important thing you have to do is fast track a bunch of free trade agreements so you can make more money with your toxic garbage — quick, before the world gets organized.

SB

Ice Cream and Doughnuts

One is cold.
One has a hole in the middle.

Cold — transform chocolate, salt, milk, sugar, fruit and ice into delicious combinations of grant money for social change organizations, for the environment. Transform a brand name *Tom and Jerry's*, for example, into ten million dollars for change this year and 1.1 million a year after that — cool. Think of the anti-globalization movement as a hub with spokes that reach out to change the world in different ways. Project Underground thwarts the mining industry. The Ruckus Society teaches people to hang from bridges, tree-sit, barricade, use cell phones for email, shut down G8 meetings. Some spokes are green and flow like gentle creeks into the mainstream. Some provide *reality tours* to vacationers who want to understand why most of the world is furious with the United States. Huge amounts of corporate funds flow from the hub to various spokes, nothing to others, insuring in-fights, ego-contests and name-calling. Eco-terrorists don't expect corporate funding but green organizations who are content with civic order get enough money to sort-of function. It's obvious that one can do more with real money than with dedicated volunteers who have no place to work, no supplies, or is it? I wonder, as I did in the sixties, why corporations would fund the anti-war movement, support radical agendas for social change, provide seed grants to radical publishers? Where is the profit in it? Were we part of their public relations budget? Or conscience money? I sort of got it the year Reagan was elected when I lost sixty-thousand grant dollars in two days — comments to the effect that multi-cultural programs *drew attention to our differences*, or in Texas, *Hell, that's just a bunch of women*. One couldn't help noticing no matter how dedicated people were, it was simply not possible to function credibly without an operating budget. That's where the Doughnuts come in. It's the name of a fund raising scheme to get money back to radical groups — lots of dough. But money is a shell game, played in the context of world financial markets driven by corporate funders whose structure we are working to dismantle. So why are they giving us money? That's where the hole comes in. Any con can tell you the game goes to the one who set it up.

That's the cold part.

SB

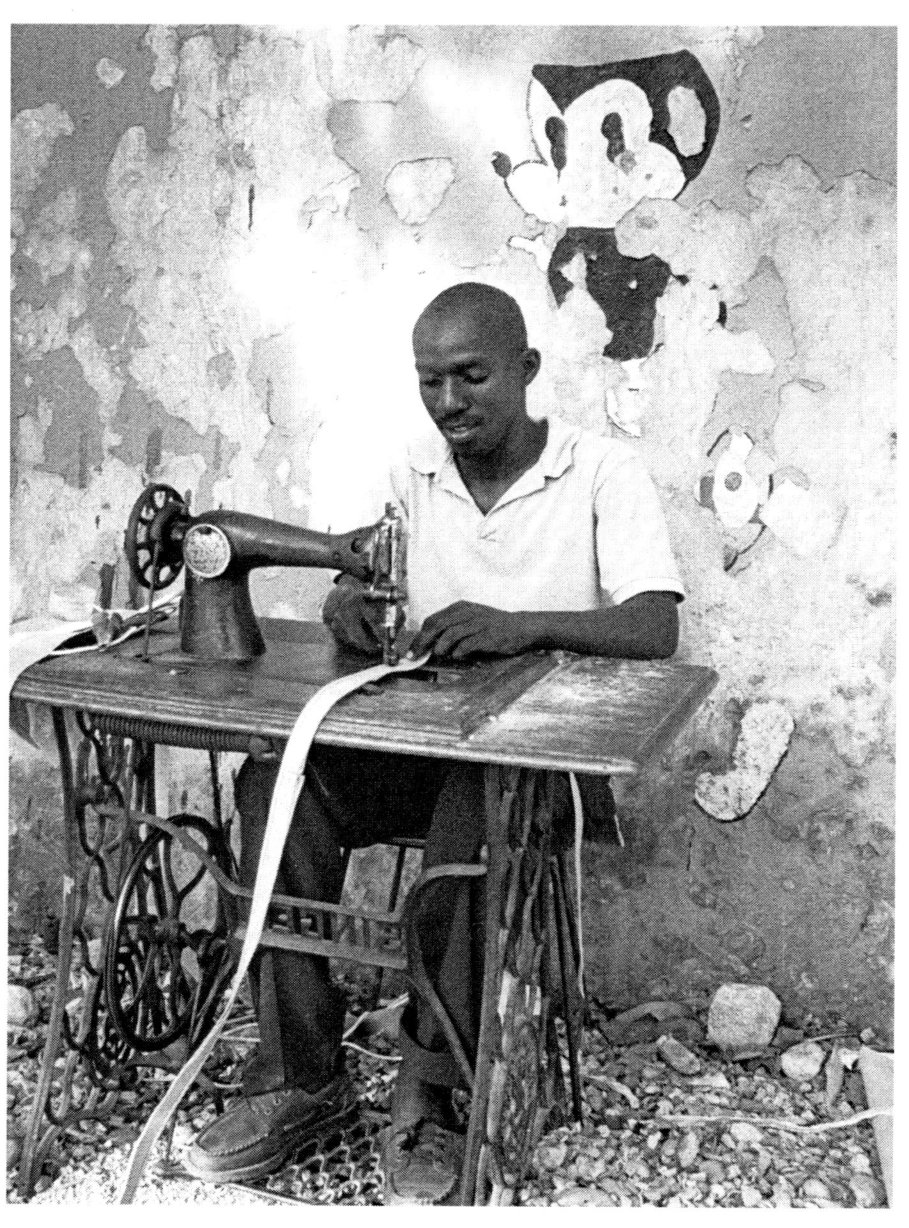

Mickey Mouse on His Shoulder, 1996, Haiti, Port-au-Prince. Man working with treadle sewing machine. Many Disney clothes are manufactured by people in Haiti who earn 34 cents an hour.

AP

Child Heart

More than 120,000, fit the number into your mind,
120,000 children, each one sucking milk from a woman,
each one laughing sometime.

All children laugh, walk for the first time, take food from a bowl
for the first time, each child is a brief hope, 120,000 of these,
each a child soldier, some as young as seven, soldiers
in the government armies of Mozambique, Angola, Burundi,
Congo-Brazzaville, the Democratic Republic of the Congo,
Liberia, Rwanda, Sierra Leone, Sudan and Uganda—
child soldiers recruited, children abducted from the school yard,
used as spies, helpers, girlfriends, boyfriends.

Victims turn to perpetrators—
children who should be playing soccer in a school yard,
play shoot-em-up, play catch with a decapitated
fifteen-year-old girl's head.

They take the names of American cartoon characters —
Daffy, Mickey Mouse, Olive, Popeye, Pluto, Elmer Fud.

More than 120,000 children. Where are their mothers?
Who are their fathers? Many as young as seven years old
easy to recruit, easy to mold into efficient weapons of war.

In America, on Hitler's birthday, two boys assassinate 12 students,
wound fifteen, plant more than 30 bombs in the high school
of a small town in Colorado.

They were imitating a video game.

Any evening, in my town, there are 3000 teenagers, armed
and pissed off, riding around town looking for someone to kill,
or beat up, in a town that doesn't know it is at war.

O child heart!

SB

Mine Fields

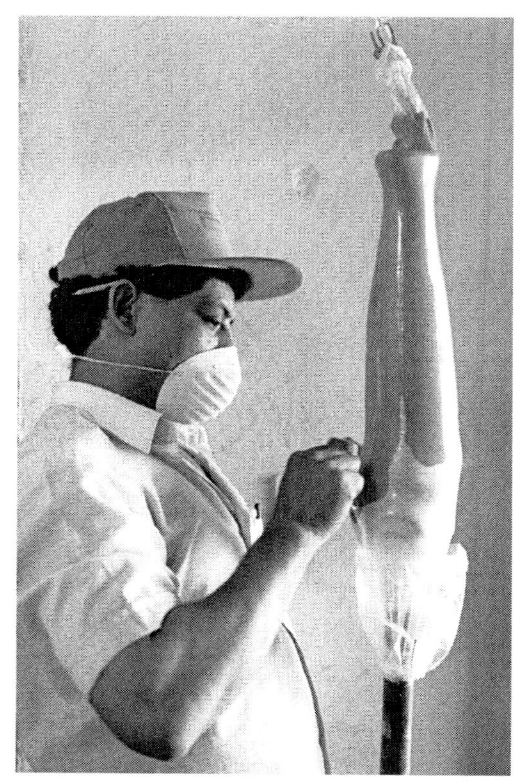

We are dropping packets of
perfectly balanced food —
lentils, peanut butter, yellow
peas and powered milk,
packaged with angel wings
attached to catch the wind,
yellow packages with
drawings that tell people the
food comes from the United
States, a nation of kind
people.

We alternate air runs,
sometimes
dropping packets of food
to feed civilians, other times
we drop scatter bombs for
military targets, except we
make mistakes —
villages get smashed and
burned, food warehouses
are demolished, international relief workers get killed.

Of course, that is to be expected.
We apologize.

Shoe stores in Afghanistan do not sell shoes in pairs
because so many people need only one
of them, one shoe —

Today we are dropping
packets of food that catch the air on angel wings,
feather down, and then alight —

on mine fields.

SB

Ahmed's Leg

His name was Ahmed Shabaan. He was 19 and lived in the village of Beit Ummar, south of Jerusalem. An Israeli army sniper shot him during clashes on the outskirts of the village. I met him when he was staying at the rehab center to get an artificial leg, the right leg. The bullet had done extensive damage to the bone and the doctors had to amputate above the knee, or was it below the knee? I don't remember.

What I remember is Ahmed's immensely handsome face, his athletic physique, and the smell of his aftershave. He was quite tall and seemed to tower me when he stood near me. He had blond hair and brown eyes. He loved to play soccer and was quite good at the sport. Now he limps wherever he goes. He will always limp wherever he goes.

I watched as they put on the artificial foot. I watched as he tried to walk. I watched as he lowered his head whenever a beautiful nurse walked by. I watched his pain. We smoked together and talked. He couldn't quite decide what he was going to do. He could no longer work as a laborer and he had already dropped out of school. Soccer was out too.

I ran into him three years later. He was walking in downtown Bethlehem. He seemed more handsome than ever. I insisted on buying him lunch. He accepted. We talked. He was drifting through life, and having a tough time dealing with his sour-tempered father. His limp was hardly visible, but I could tell because I knew. He invited me to visit his family, but I knew I wouldn't go. I invited him to visit me, but I knew he wouldn't come.

We both reminded one another of the doctors and the rehabilitation center and the artificial limbs. I reminded him why he couldn't play soccer anymore. He reminded me of why I hated the occupation.

(Photograph preceding page) **The Leg Maker**, 1996, San Salvador. An FMLN wounded veteran coats a lower leg with plastic at a small prosthetics factory. *MH*

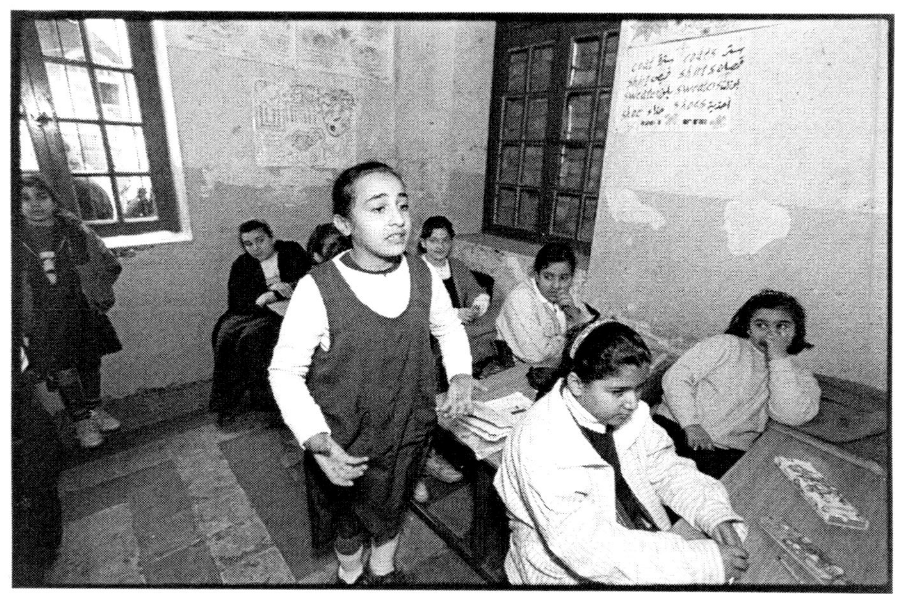

School Girl, Dijla School for girls, Baghdad. 1998.

After four days of solid bombing this girl addressed our delegation: "When you go back to America ask the children to tell the parents not to bomb us." She returned to her desk and cried.

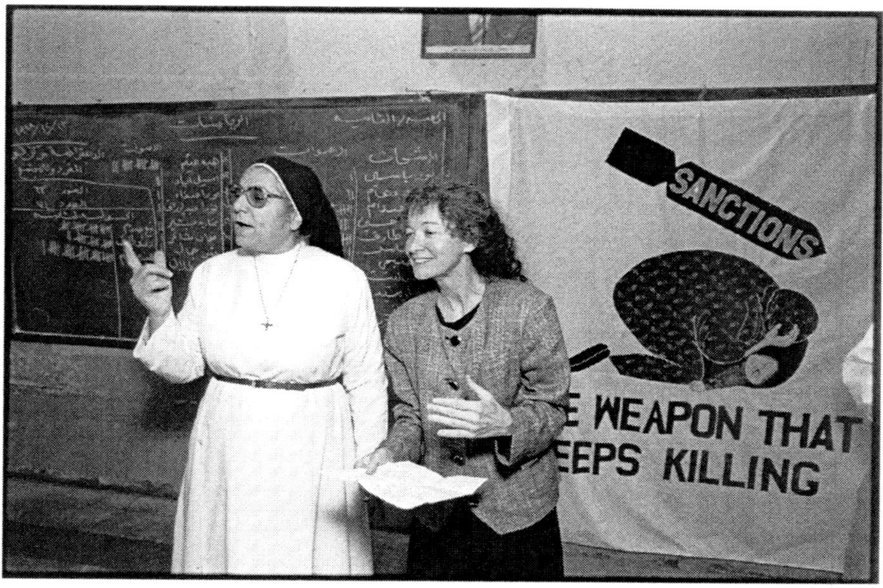

We Shall Overcome, 1998, Baghdad. Sister Susanne, principal of the school and Kathy Kelley, of Voices in the Wilderness, teaching the children "We Shall Overcome" in Arabic. *AP*

Dijla School for Girls

Americans rarely come here.
The children have something to say.

A large banner proclaims:
Sanctions: the weapon that keeps killing.

A lesson in Arabic is elegant
on the chalkboard,
a row of tallies marks the place
mathematics was invented.

Ten-year-old girls —
warm clothing, western dress.

This is a catholic school —
chipped paint,
one window boarded up.

These children have lived
under sanctions their whole lives,
are ambassadors for a people exiled
from the world.

They are strong children
whose less fortunate
and more fragile friends
and family members
have not survived.

One girl stands up to speak —
When you return to America
ask the children to tell their parents
not to bomb us.

I told her I would do it, Alan said.

SB

The Classroom

We went to film them in the classroom. It was April or May 1994. The place was the School for Boys, run by the United Nations Works and Relief Agency (UNRWA) in Shati Refugee Camp in Gaza. The boys in the classroom were about 11 or 12 years old.

It was about 10:30 in the morning.

"How many of you participated in demonstrations against Israel's occupation army?" I asked as the camera rolled.

The entire classroom raised their hands.

"How many of you threw stones at the armed soldiers?"

The entire classroom raised their hands.

"How many of you were shot by a soldier?"

Two-thirds of the classroom raised their hands.

"How many of you were shot more than once?"

A bit less than half the classroom raised their hands. They started lifting their t-shirts and pulling up their pants to show me — and the camera — their bullet-wound scars. Everyone laughed when one boy said he was shot in the ass and asked me if I wanted to see. I smiled.

"How many of you had a family member arrested by the soldiers?"

The entire classroom raised their hands.

"How many of you were beaten by the soldiers?"

The entire classroom raised their hands.

"How many of you had a family member shot dead by the soldiers?"

One-third of the classroom raised their hands.

This was after the first Palestinian uprising, which started on December 9, 1987 and lasted for 7 years. Are any of these boys alive this uprising around? Will any of them live to show their wounds?

MH

(photograph facing page) **Dying Children**

Al Mansour Children's Hospital, Bagdhad, 2000. A mother watches over her dying son. The relative high cost of medication makes treatment impossible for this and other Iraqi children suffering from leukemia. According to UNICEF, 4,500 Iraqis, of which half are children under the age of five, die each month from hunger and disease. To date more than half of a million Iraqi children under the age of five have died as a direct result of U.S. sanctions.

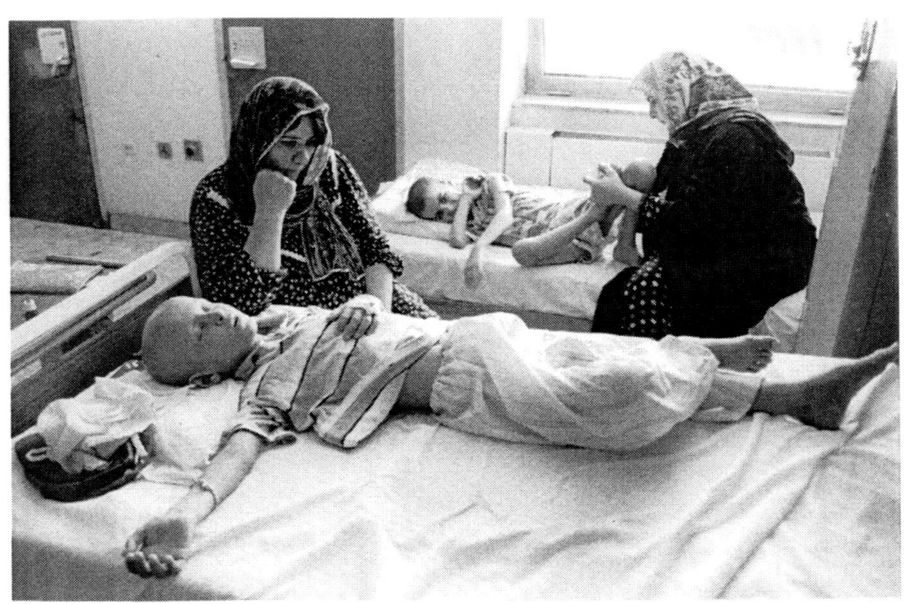

Dying Children

I know about this.
My brother died of leukemia.
One small death after millions of deaths in WWII —
One small death that ripped my parents hearts,
their lives, my child soul to shreds.
I think about this every day.

I see two small boys in an Iraqi hospital.
One mother watches a child, who looks like my son, while he sleeps.
She purifies each blood cell with mother love in her mind.
There are too many bad cells.

Later she will wring her hands, search, search, search
for something she should have done — and didn't know to do.
Another mother rubs her child's foot and tries to make him laugh.
Leukemia can be cured. We have medicine.

They do not.

SB

Who Bought the Milk for the Baby?

The year was 1994. The place was Shifa Hospital in Gaza. I was there with a film crew, working on a documentary for Channel 4 TV in London about the Palestinian-Israeli conflict. They kept all the brain-dead patients in one section of the hospital. They were all young men who were shot in the head by Israeli soldiers. I don't remember what we went there to film, but we came across this young man. I think his name was Al'a and he was in his mid or late twenties. He was on his way to buy milk for his baby girl. There was a demonstration and the soldiers were firing live ammunition at the demonstrators.. Al'a stuck his head out from behind a wall to see if the coast was clear so he could cross the street to the store. The bullet hit him in the head and he fell down. I remember watching the scene on TV. It was a famous incident and everyone talked about it for a while to come. I remember from the TV footage that Al'a was wearing a black leather jacket that day. I had no idea I would see him in person one day.

For the nearly six to eight months that we were filming in Gaza, I would go see Ala' in the hospital every time I had a chance. My friend Joumah took me. I cried each time because I felt so helpless. Ala' just laid there, like a spoiled vegetable, and I couldn't do anything for him. His body was like a skeleton and his wife and his brother would take turns changing him, cleaning him and taking care of him. His brother had an electric appliance repair shop. He lost business because he spent too much time at the hospital and his shop was closed most of the time. Ala's wife seemed like she was in her early twenties. She would come to the hospital, sit by her husband's bed and tell him the latest news about their child, his parents, her parents, and the neighborhood where they lived. Al'a never budged. He never opened his eyes. After a year a half, maybe more, he died. He lost his life, just like that, while on his way to buy milk for his baby girl. His brother called me and told me the news. In a way, I was relieved. I felt relieved for the wife and the brother. Watching them spend their days and nights at the hospital bed was so sad. They knew Ala' could never recover, but the brother kept hoping. He took Ala' to Egypt for treatment. He didn't want to give up hope, even though there was no hope.

I wonder what his baby girl looks like now. She is about seven years old. Does she look like Ala'? Did her mother tell her he was shot on the way to buy her milk? And what about his brother? Did he open his shop again? Did he find a new husband for his sister-in-law? Or has she remained a widow to this day?

And on the day when Ala' was shot, who ended up buying the milk for his hungry baby girl?

MH

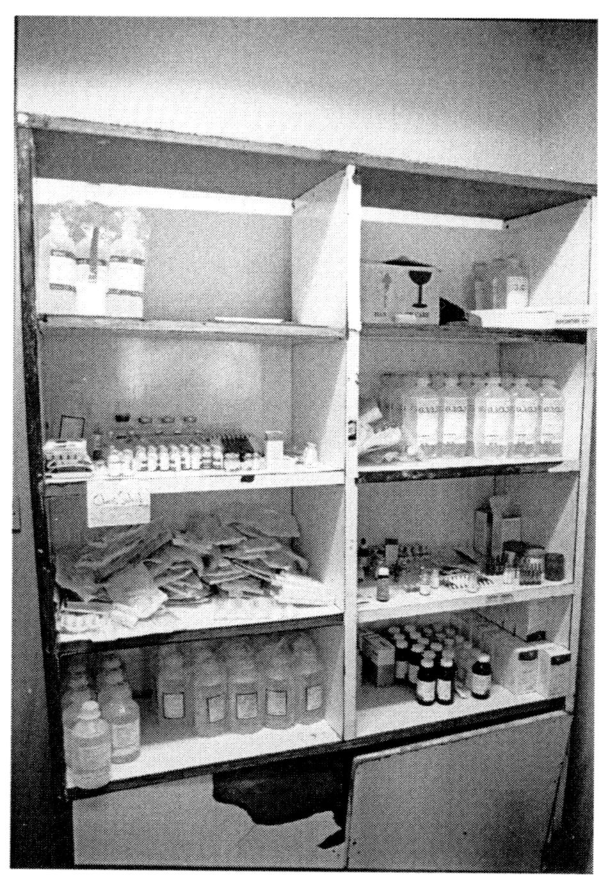

The pharmacy is in the Pediatric and Maternity Hospital in Basra. There are 1.6 million people in Basra. The P & M hospital is a large one, second only to the general hospital, like Brackenridge and the children's wing. Dr. Ferros Adul Abass, the head resident physician, like all Iraqi doctors, studied medicine in English. He explained that children can die from the lack of the simplest drug. Children with diarrhea develop a high concentration of acid in their blood. For the lack of bicarbonate of soda they die. More expensive anti-leukemia medicines either are not there or the pharmacy lacks the full complement of them. The hospital also lacks small breathing and feeding tubes, oxygen tanks, special bags for collecting blood for their blood bank, and many more items which are taken for granted in the United States. The hospital buildings are large modern structures. The doctors are highly trained. Many of the doctors did their post graduate work in the United States, England and France. Their frustration is tremendous. They keep a brave face for their patients and then go to their offices to cry. *AP*

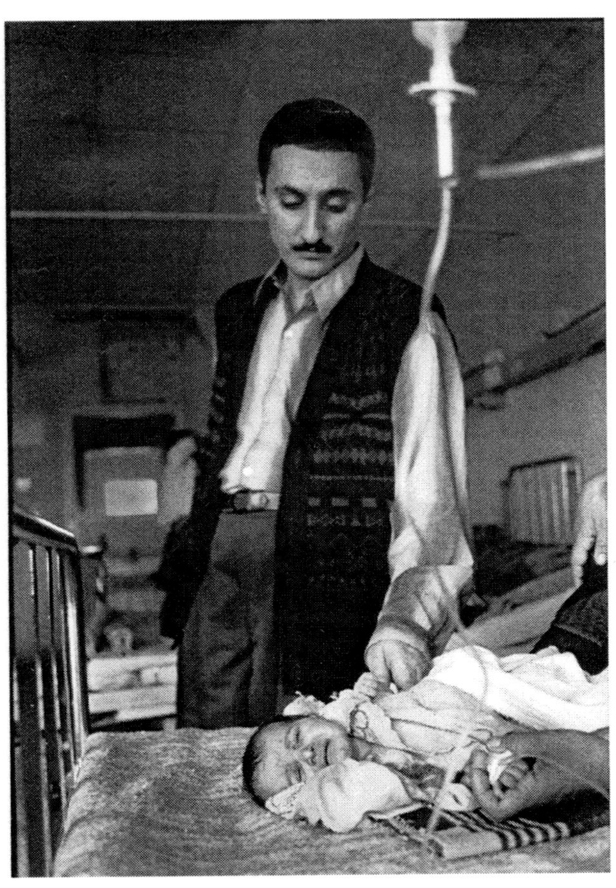

Dr. Abbas

Basra Maternity and Pediatric Hospital. 1998.

A lack of medicine leaves head resident physician Dr. Abbas, and other doctors like him, powerless to treat his patients. This infant is anemic and will likely die.

Dr. Abass could leave Iraq as thousands have. He has a marketable skill, as they say. He is frustrated every day by the lack of resources but he knows that if he leaves even more mothers and babies will die. He cannot leave. I remember the Jewish school principal in Germany during WWII who heard that the students of his school were to be rounded up and taken to a concentration camp. He could have run away. He went to the concentration camp with his students. He could not leave them.

AP

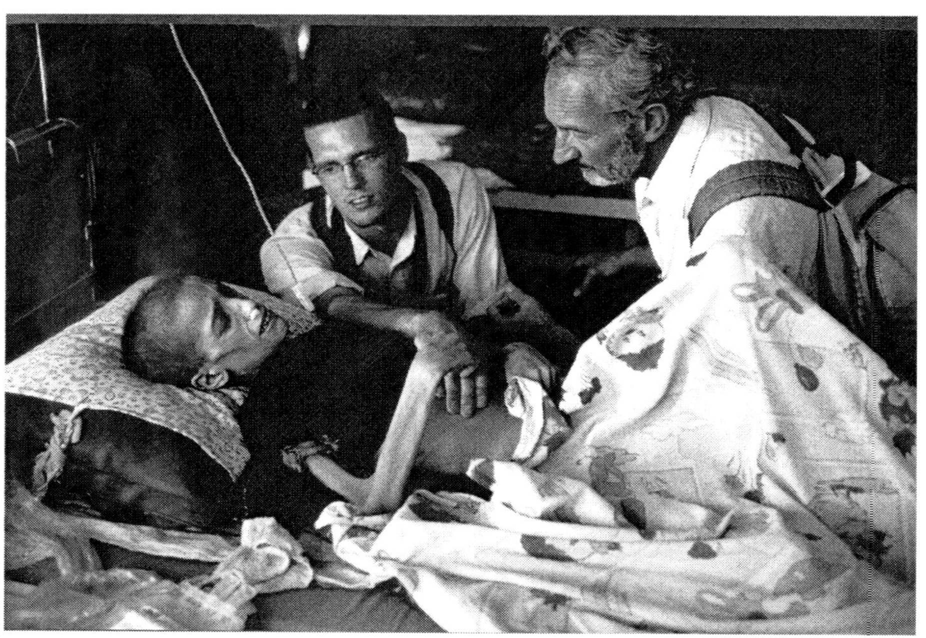

Kamal Dying
Bagdhad, August, 2000.
The relatiavely high cost of medication makes treatment impossible for this and other Iraqi children dying from leukemia. (L to R)-Kamal, Phil Steger, Bert Sacks — members of Voices from the Wilderness.

AP

Seeing It

If I could dismiss the waste —

I would say people go to hospitals
when they are sick or dying.

I would say I have seen people
waste to air in the Unites States.
AIDS or cancer can suck muscle,
can suck tissue out, can flatten bones.

I would say maybe it is something no one
could help.

I would sit with Alan a long time –
convince him he did not see what he saw.

It would take a very, very, very —
long time to talk Alan out of
what he sees.

When he snaps a photo of the world
it is true.

Cartoon characters on a flannel blanket.

I nod, close my eyes,
open them again.

And weep.

SB

A Flashlight Brightens the Intifada

It was an emotionally draining afternoon. I had spent a few hours at Al-Makassed Hospital in East Jerusalem, which handles the most serious Intifada injuries. As usual, as I walked out of the hospital, I took a deep sense of depression and disgust with me.

Palestinians of all ages and both sexes lie in their hospital beds with every type of bullet injury imaginable. Many have been shot in the back and have been paralyzed for life. A doctor pulls back the sheets from their legs and shows me how their feet are turned inward, motionless. Others have been shot in the leg and are recovering from amputations. The doctor pulls back the sheets again. One has had his leg amputated from the thigh, another from above the knee, another from below the knee and yet another from above the ankle.

There are some who were shot in the eye and had it surgically removed. An entire "Intifada Ward" at Al-Makassed is filled with these scenes of human misery.

Pride, Pain and Boredom

Most touching of all are the eyes of the Intifada patients. They look at me with pride because they don't want any pity; pain because they know their physical handicaps are permanent; and boredom because they are accustomed to visitors who come to look at their wounds, say a few kind words and then leave without offering any solutions for their individual problems as victims, or their collective problem as an oppressed nation.

The first time I saw 15-year-old Omar, however, his eyes were closed. It was April 14, 1989, and he was laying unconscious in the intensive care unit. Earlier in the day, Israel's notorious Border Police had entered his West Bank village of Nahalin, massacring its unarmed residents. Altogether, five Palestinians were killed and more than 30 wounded. Omar was shot as he was leaving the mosque after the dawn prayer, and the bullet penetrated his right kidney. It was removed shortly after he was brought to Al-Makassed hospital. A few hours after his operation, when I first saw him, tubes extended from his nose, mouth and arms and the doctors were not sure he would survive.

Two weeks later, I was back at Al-Makassed. Omar was conscious and lying on his back. Dr. Wahib Dajani, head of ICU, explained to me that the single bullet had cost Omar his right kidney and also passed very close to his spinal cord, permanently paralyzing him in both legs, then punctured his left kidney.

I looked at Omar's face, his eyes glazed with pain, and wanted to cry. He whispered something; and an elderly man, who was standing by his bed side, lowered his head to Omar's ear. Saliva was dripping from the boy's mouth, and he wanted the man to wipe it away. The later did so with the utmost attention and care.

"Who is that man?" I asked Dr. Dajani.

"Omar's father," he replied. "He has never left the hospital since Omar was brought here." I had been too absorbed watching Omar to notice that both his father and mother were standing silently by his bed.

"The mother comes early each morning," Dr. Dajani continued, "and then goes back to Nahalin at the end of the day."

I looked at Um Omar, but I was lost for words. What could I say to a mother whose eldest son was shot in cold blood? Would she believe me if I told her that justice will prevail someday? Would I believe myself?

Overwhelmed by how sad Omar and his parents looked, I was not strong enough to stay with them any longer. It was almost five in the afternoon and Dr. Dajani, whom I had come to know well during my visits, offered me a lift home after he completed his rounds.

When we finally left, Dr. Dajani spotted Um Omar by the side of the road, waiting for the bus. He pulled the car over and offered her a ride. Um Omar thanked him, got in the car and we rode off toward Bethlehem. Too exhausted and depressed to talk, I remained silent as we drove out of Jerusalem. But it was hard to take my eyes off Um Omar. She was in her thirties, had very pretty green eyes, dark lashes and one of the most serene faces I had ever seen. I heard her mumbling something under her breath and her sadness broke my heart.

"What will happen to Omar?" I finally asked her.

Turning her head slowly and speaking in a whisper, she said, "I cannot think about what is going to happen. I live with Omar's situation one day at a time and everyday I pray to God that he is not in a lot of pain."

"But what about the future?" I persisted. "Did the doctor say that Omar will be able to walk again?"

"I don't ask them about the future," she replied. "I am not sure I can handle thinking past today."

Trying to change the subject, I told her that I had been to her village, Nahalin, nearly two weeks earlier.

She seemed interested, so I told her about my visit to interview the villagers about the massacre. I had to hike to Nahalin because the Israeli military had put huge boulders on the roads to prevent people from going in and out of the village.

"The hike was more than two kilometers long and I was exhausted from the heat," I explained. "When it was time to leave in the afternoon, I knew I could not walk through the hills again. I asked the villagers if I could hire a donkey. At first they laughed, but when they realized I was serious, they found a donkey for me. And with a group of kids in tow, I rode out of Nahalin."

"Are you a writer?" Um Omar asked.

"Yes," I answered, surprised by her question.

"One day, when I returned home from the hospital, my 10-year-old son, Alaa', told me that he gave a visiting writer a ride to the next village on our donkey." she explained. "He was really upset because when she tried to thank him with some money and a small flashlight, an older kid ordered him not to take anything. So it was you?"

"Your son gave me the ride?" I asked, finding the coincidence hard to believe.

For the first time since we met, Um Omar smiled. "Yes, it was Alaa' and you should have seen how upset he was about the flashlight. He said it had a pretty color, yellow or something."

"Listen," I told her, "when you get home tonight, give Alaa' my greetings and tell him that God meant for him to have the flashlight after all." And with this, I pulled the flashlight out of my bag and handed it to her.

Um Omar smiled fleetingly, and the cloud of depression that had hovered over my head since we left the hospital lifted. The flashlight suddenly symbolized everything that was pure, good and gentle. Just for a moment, it was alleviated — my feeling of impotence and uselessness over my inability to do something for Omar and his mother, to snatch away the flood of their human pain and suffering.

The Washington Report on Middle East Affairs, February 1990

MH

(photograph proceeding page) **Paradise Hotel,** Bethlehem, 2001.

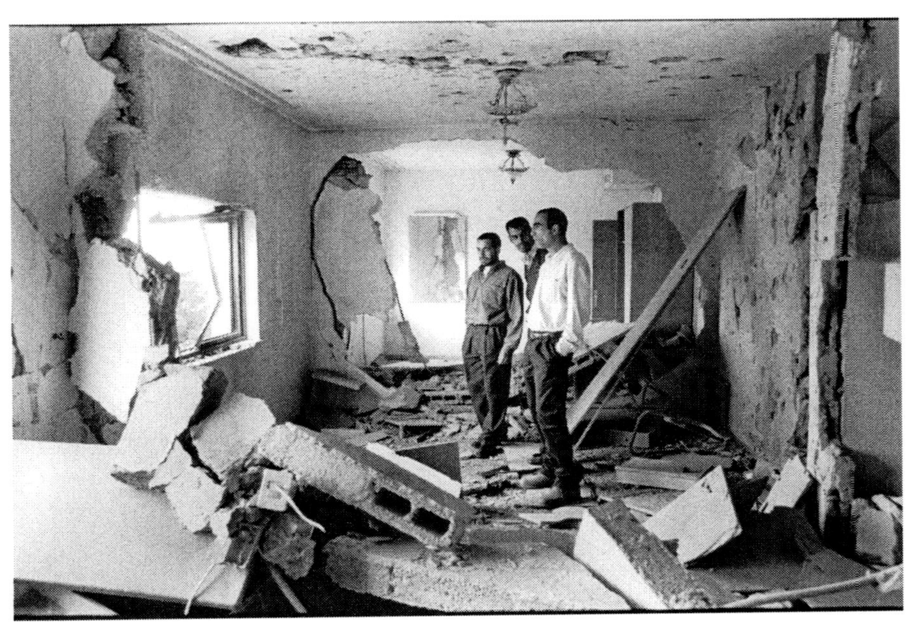

Paradise Hotel

It was bombed before and we built it up again.
I have this on video tape, he said.
George in an engineer who returned
to the Paradise Hotel because his *visa* ran out —
his company didn't want to lose him so they
filled out paperwork and held his job while
he waited to come back.
In the meantime he had nothing to do but make videos
of the new damage.

This time they destroyed the entire front of the building
and the building across the street and around the corner.
George is perhaps thirty years old.
He has come to an opening of Alan's photographs.

On the porch later someone asks him if he
is one of the men in the photograph.
No, he says, *But my mother taught two of them in school,*
and their children.

AP, SB

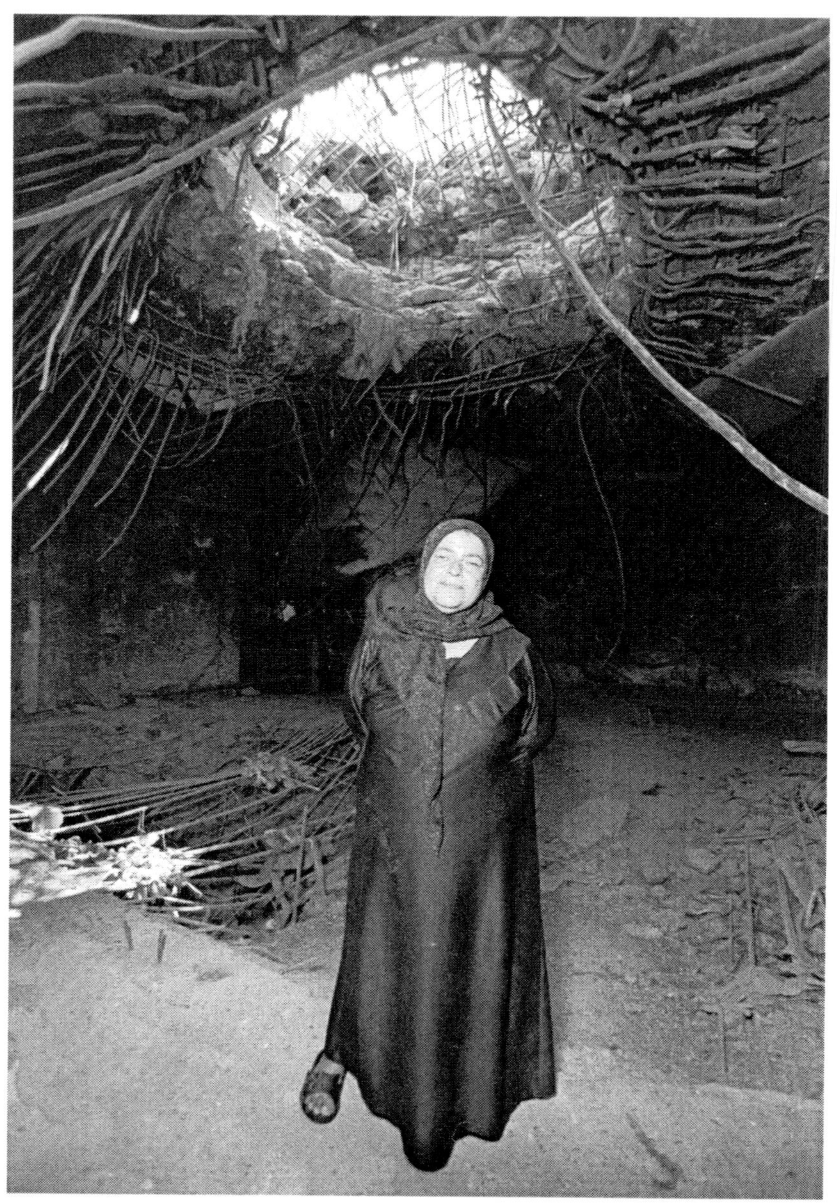

Civilian Bomb Shelter

Amariya civilian bomb shelter, Baghdad, 1998. Four hundred and nineteen Iraqis, mostly women and children, died here in 1991 when two U.S. smart bombs penetrated the six foot reinforced walls. Our guide, Nahia Kazol Mahady, lives near here, where she was an elementary school teacher for 25 years. She is now pursuing a doctorate in Philosophy. *AP*

School of the World

Small girls walk to school in Belfast through a gauntlet of jeering adults who throw stones at children, wear grotesque rubber masks, images of the Queen, Halloween ghouls, less horrific perhaps as the people who smeared each other and the walls of their prison with their own feces, or used Makita power drills to the brain to execute (they needed to save bullets) a shop keeper, or someone with the wrong opinion, god, litany, church service — I don't remember which side committed which outrage. We don't remember the reason because there can be no justification for atrocity. God, of course, may not agree. He shows up on the side of violent behavior as regularly as Freedom does, in one pocket a revolutionary agenda, in another, oppression, jack, queen, hearts, diamonds, bad luck to be born to violent circumstance. Like fingers in a glove, Good v. Evil slip into our rhetoric, into the words we use to think with and we're back on the street dodging explosions. Small girls on their way to school in Belfast are part of the dialectic. Someone is frustrated because they cannot have their way, an outrage has occurred, another, another, another, until it spirals down to a Vietnamese child on fire running naked down the road, a street execution, death camps, lampshades made from human skin, Palestinian children blown up on their way to school, Israeli children at a pizza parloutr murdered by a suicide bomber. An infant dies from anemia because its homeland has been cordoned off, no medicine, bad water. Small boys bow and hunker, back and forth like someone vomiting or being raped by an idea, a word, a dichotomy, *Good v. Evil.* The School of the World imprints *the idiot* onto child souls — who cannot understand the trick of it, how in a dichotomy of *Good* and *Evil* there is no *Good,* how *Good* lives in the midst of complex shadows, consists of shining jewels in each heart called — forgiveness, problem-solving, compassion, tolerance, love. Small girls, in red uniforms, tall socks, rosy cheeks aflame, green eyes, duck ghouls throwing stones in Belfast on their way to school, fire bombs on the street. Someone stands on a smoking mass grave, fists raised to the sky declares war on Evil-doers, retaliation, now — the School of the World.

SB

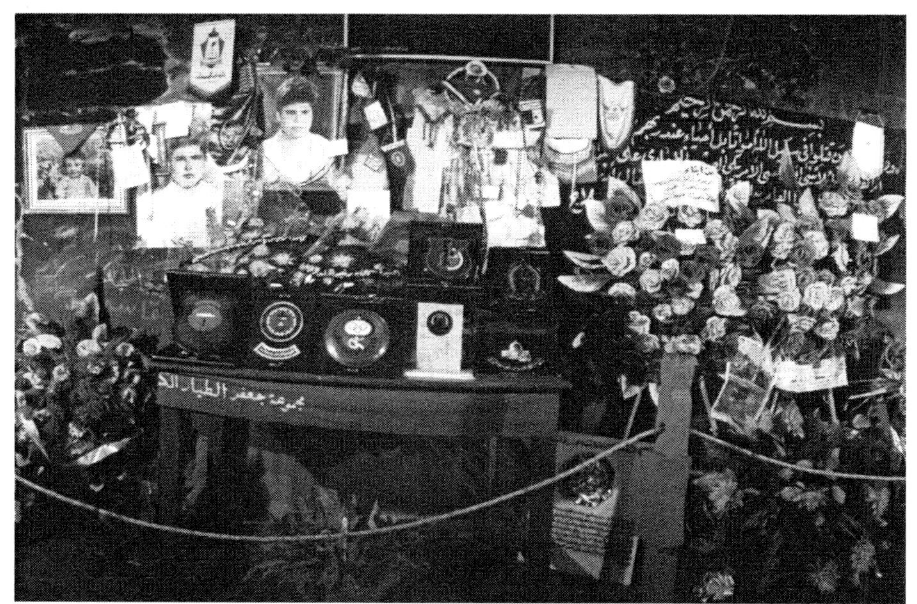

Memorial to the Dead, Amariya Shelter, Baghdad, Iraq, 2000

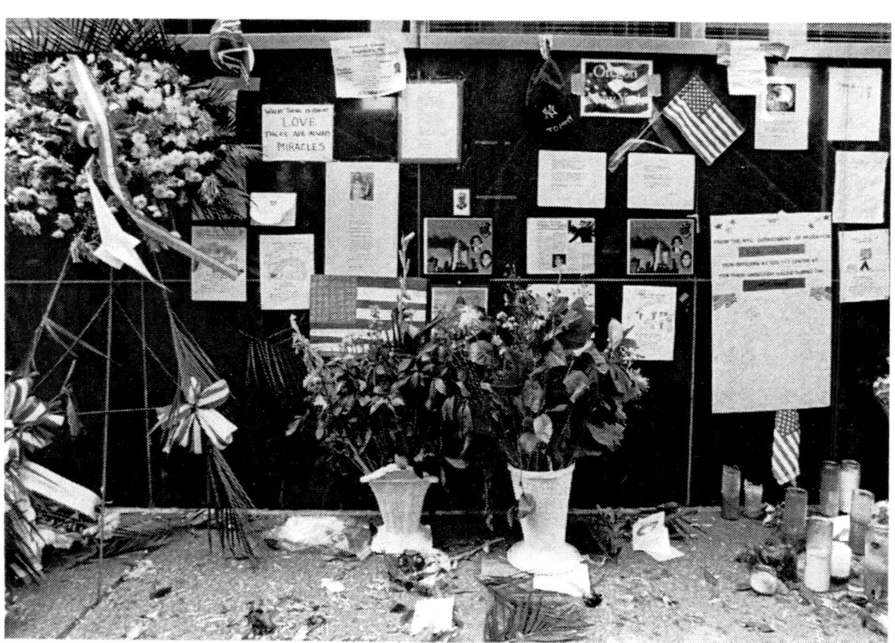

Memorial to the Dead, New York, USA, 2001.

AP

The Layers of Our Seeing

At first I see Nahia Kazol Mahady
in Alan's photograph
standing beneath a hole
in a cold universe.
Later I find another print
of the Amariya shelter
where 419 human beings
were killed by smart missiles
in 1991 —

And the cold universe
becomes a shrine —

Persian letters
and photographs of children
and their mothers, plaques
and plastic flowers, roses
covered in plastic to keep them
fresh, the plaid head scarf women wear,
a baseball cap that says *Tommy*,
and *New York*,
letters in every language,
medallions and prayer beads,
funeral arrangements of flowers,
votive candles, one small
plastic flower against bomb rubble,
acres of candles, a stand of
carnations, snap shots of the missing
pasted onto a laser print
of the twin towers, smoking,
table scarves, a picture of the president,
a teenage boy with dream-eyes,
a child's drawing of her father,
who worked in the twin towers,
a darling toddler
posed in front of a bank

of flowers, perhaps a photographer's
banner. Alan said he couldn't think
of anywhere in Iraq one would
find flowers like that, a Frisbee,
a poem wrapped in plastic,
an American flag, another one,
presents, gift wrapped,
that will never be opened,
a conch shell, a handwritten
page that says *Where there is*
Great Love there are always miracles,
the Koran, the Bible, business
cards with messages written
across the back, a round fan,
a veil, a star, a wrinkled
picture of a baby.

The cold universe
becomes a shrine as the layers
of our seeing unfold like
rose petals in the
slant light of September.

SB

Collective Punishment

Dheisheh Refugee Camp — It was shortly after 1 p.m. on Wednesday, July 30, when I walked to a friend's house for a quick visit. I found Um Naim and her daughter-in-law sitting cross-legged on the floor, patiently filling a stack of grape leaves with rice and meat stuffing.

"Did you hear what happened?" Um Naim asked me after we greeted each other. "Two bombs went off at the Mahaneh Yehuda market in West Jerusalem," she said, directing my attention to the live Israeli TV coverage that they had apparently been watching when I came in. "My daughter Amal is at work at Maqassed Hospital," she added. "I hope she'll get back from Jerusalem safely."

"Oh my God! How is my husband going to get home?" I gasped in panic. "Is Ahmed in Ramallah?" Um Naim asked. "The Israelis just clamped a closure on the Palestinian areas and gave Palestinians until 7 o'clock tonight to leave Israel," she explained, "but I am sure there are no checkpoints on the Wadi Nar [Valley of Fire] road" — a winding mountainous road which is the only remaining access road between the northern and southern West Bank without driving through Israel.

Too worried to sit still, I went home. On the way, I stopped next door to tell my neighbors the news. Ra'ed and his family were watching television, or at least trying to.

"Did your son Firas come back from work?" I asked Ra'ed's mother. She shook her head, distraught. "He's working at a settlement near Hebron," she said. "He doesn't have a work permit and if he gets caught by the soldiers, they'll probably beat him to a pulp." And Um Ra'ed's brother and two nephews work in West Jerusalem not far from the Mahaneh Yehuda market. "They just called us and said that the place is swarming with soldiers and police and they can't leave. My brother has a work permit but my nephews don't," Um Ra'ed said apprehensively.

I was invited to stay for lunch. At 3:30 p.m., just as we were finishing, my husband's car pulled up. Ahmed had left his Ramallah office at 1:30 P.M. without knowing anything about the explosions. "While I was driving on the Wadi Nar road, I was told by some drivers that there was an Israeli checkpoint at the entrance of Beit Sahour and cars were being sent back to Ramallah," Ahmed explained. "But I kept going, and after we were held at the checkpoint for over an hour, they let the cars through."

In addition to sealing off the Palestinian self-rule areas from Israel, the Israelis announced that Palestinian movement is prohibited between

Areas A, B and C of the Palestinian territories. So 65,000 Palestinians who work inside Israel and the thousands who work in the self-rule areas had to face numerous Israeli army checkpoints before reaching their homes.

Within a few hours of the bombings, the Bethlehem checkpoint into Jerusalem was a sight to see: Israeli soldiers were stopping all Palestinian cars arriving from Jerusalem. All identity cards were being rigorously checked. Those with permits to enter Israel and Jerusalem were let go; those without were gathered at a nearby parking lot. Hundreds of Palestinians were rounded up and detained until midnight. All had to find a way of getting home. Some lived in Areas B and C in Bethlehem and the rest lived in Hebron and its surrounding villages.

Palestinians who did have permits had a difficult time as well. After crossing the checkpoint, they were stopped at a second checkpoint at the village of al-Khader. Using the pretext that al-Khader is in Area C, soldiers would not allow the workers to pass.

By early evening, scores of Palestinian workers were sitting by the side of the road near Dheisheh Camp trying to figure out what to do. Camp residents suggested putting them up for the night, but everyone knew better: finding their way home the following morning would be even tougher since the closure was expected to be tightened even further. And so, the workers climbed walls, jumped off cliffs, and walked miles on treacherous dirt roads to get where they needed to go.

Firas and his friends hid until 3 p.m. at the construction site in the Hebron settlement where he works. When they felt it was safe to leave, they hopped inside a car and drove through dirt roads bypassing checkpoints until they reached the Bethlehem village of Hussan. From there, they took another car which drove them to Dheisheh. It took them nearly three and a half hours longer than usual to arrive, but they did get home.

The following morning, Firas went back to work. He had a job to finish and no checkpoint was going to deter him. "What if the soldiers had caught you?" I asked him when he returned. "So what? I would have gotten a beating; it wouldn't be the first time," he said.

Um Ra'ed's nephews, who were stuck at their job site in West Jerusalem, waited until 8:30 in the evening before they felt it was safe to leave. They called an East Jerusalem taxi which picked them up and dropped them off past the Gilo tunnel near Beit Jala. They arrived home at 10:30 p.m.

Other workers were not so lucky. A van loaded with laborers was stopped at a Palestinian security checkpoint near al-Khader. According to Imad, a Bethlehem man working with Palestinian intelligence, the driver of the van looked as if he was in a daze, with his head swaying back and forth. "He told us that they were workers driving back from Hebron when they were stopped and beaten by Israeli soldiers at a checkpoint." Imad said he felt sorry for the men, some of whom looked as if they had been beaten quite badly.

Early the next morning, I heard banging at my front gate. It was a woman from the village of al-Khader selling grapes. "How did you get past the checkpoints?" I asked her. "I took a detour," she laughed. "Weren't you afraid of getting caught?" I persisted. "Allah will help," she said, "and if I don't sell my grapes, they will go bad." A few hours later, a small pick-up truck drove past my house. "Fresh Jericho watermelons," the driver spoke through a loudspeaker. Another person with guts out to make a living.

"People try to go about their business, it just takes them longer to get it done when there is a closure," said Mohammed, a cigarette distributor who drove from Hebron through back roads for two and a half hours in order to make his deliveries in Bethlehem.

"Did you go to Beit Jala near the Israeli bypass road?" he asked me. I said I hadn't. "Go look," he smiled. "The Israeli soldiers have sealed off the road which leads to the bypass with a pile of dirt. But as we speak, Israeli food delivery trucks are parked on the Israeli side and the drivers are throwing cartons of food over to the Palestinian distributors on the other side."

This story was confirmed by Nader, who owns a supermarket in Bethlehem. "Take a look," he said, "we had fresh Israeli bread delivered today as well as dairy products. Nothing is in short supply because the Israelis will benefit from doing business."

How many Palestinians will be able to buy these foods is another story altogether. As the closure drags on, belts will be tightened more than they already are. This current closure comes at the end of the month, when everyone was waiting to get paid. So families will eat lentils today, tomorrow, and the day after.

The residents of Dheisheh say they hate every minute of it just as they hate all aspects of the closure, collective punishment and Israel's unjust policies. But they are determined not to let it break them.

The day of the bombing, a wedding took place in Dheisheh. The families of the bride and groom sang and danced late into the night. In another house, some children were singing along to a new hit Egyptian video clip called "Apple of my Eye." I stopped to watch. The children were grinning, their dark eyes bright with laughter.

The closure may have dried up their pocket money and taken their food consumption down to the bare essentials. Yet the spirit is there — very much there. It is the same spirit which has year after year since 1948 faced up to Israeli military might and shouted, "We are alive...alive...alive...".

Palestine Report — August 8, 1997

MH

Don’t Say America

After she spoke of American colonialism, military bases in Turkey and elsewhere, she said I wasn’t to say *America* when I meant the U.S. because Peru was also America. Sadness tugged my heart, something about identity, something lost in the translation, a European defining me. And I might agree, except when I think of who I am, American comes to mind, not U.S. which is government, military bases, income tax, no one—political parties. *United States* is administration, a war machine. America has soft sounds, vowels like fertile ground, something to plant in, corn growing, and coyotes along the road, sun glinting into windows, Lake Michigan, New Mexico at twilight, the *Rio De Los Animus Perdidos* that rides low clouds along the continental divide, the Mississippi river in Minnesota, where you can step across a clear green stream, my mother’s voice singing as she moves into her nineties. I criticize the United States, complain at its idiocy, but cannot deny America — her wild song is my breath. She is the heart of us, with her vast carpet bag of errors, errors that she learned from European mothers and fathers. Argentineans do not call themselves Americans. They might relate to being *South American*. Canadians don’t say they are *Americans*, some aren’t even Canadian. El Salvadorans might say they are *Central Americans* but wouldn’t call themselves *American*, unless they came here, like everyone else, for refuge. Last night I dreamed Kalamu ya Salaam and Joan of Arc were at my high school reunion in Illinois. Everyone else was a stranger, except my son, who was always out of reach. My son is an American teenager. He was also a Native American orphan and a child of war. We are not strangers to the chaos of the human soul, nor did we invent it, nor is it American, or German, or French, or English, Spanish, Portuguese or Dutch, Russian or Chinese. America is a *mestizo* learning how to heal the violence of her heritage. Sometimes she is an old ballad, apple pie, a back road to the creek. The U.S., that’s another thing entirely, anonymous — an abused child of colonialism who repeats, repeats, repeats the cycle. But America is a mother whose soul is a clear river flowing, cascading across the tall mountain spine of modern life, and where there is a river there is growth.

SB

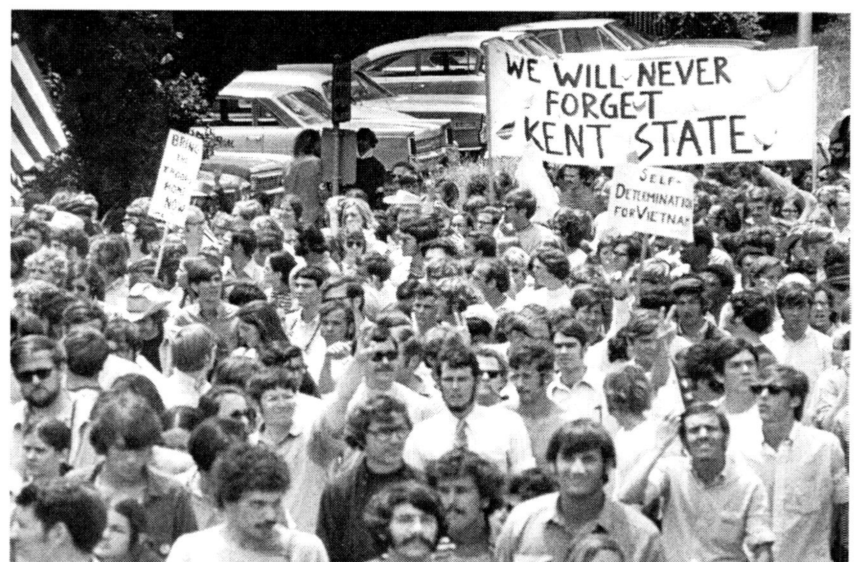

Anti-War March, Austin, early 1970. The largest peace march ever in Austin, over twenty thousand people, marching in response to the illegal bombing of Cambodia and the murder of students at Kent State and in Jackson Mississippi where black students in their dormitory rooms were shot and killed.

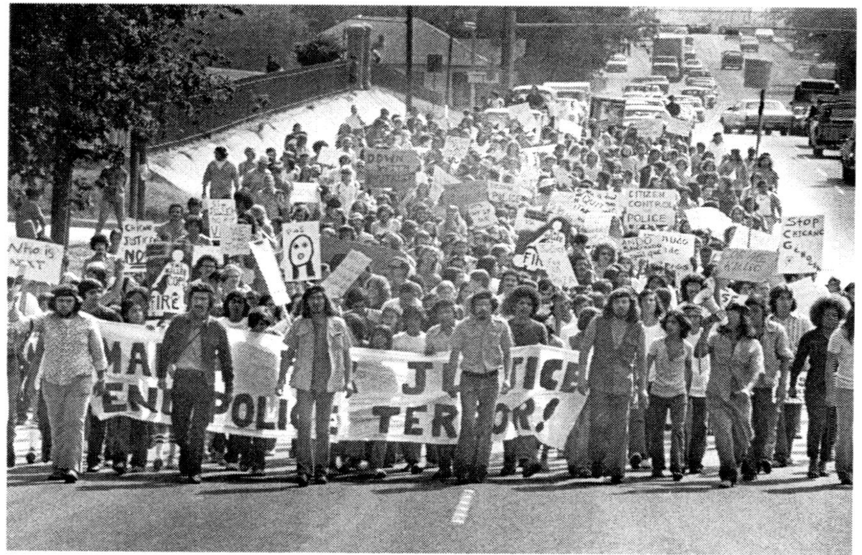

Justice, 1974, East Austin, TX. A march against police brutality led by the Brown Berets.

AP

Mosquito

Five hundred thousand people in Italy march to protest military strikes in Afghanistan, a hundred thousand in London. Protesters in Paris, Frankfurt, Indonesia, Australia, and in Washington D.C. create a street version of the United Nations, every imaginable interest group — free Leonard Peltier, Korean Women against War Crimes. Relief workers say millions of human beings could die from starvation and exposure in Afghanistan this winter. Socialists attack western imperialism, unions remind us human beings have a right to jobs. Christians, Muslims, atheists, students, teachers, feminists, environmental activists, the Black Bloc, tree sitters, bridge hangers, people whose political visions differ profoundly come together to confront the warrior class. As world leaders rush to a clash of civilizations, radical agendas vie for recognition in a raucous exercise in coalition building. Some want violent overthrow, confrontation, no more atrocity. Some declare a huge foul. To fly commercial airplanes into skyscrapers breaks the rules of a world game we have agreed to. But everyone did not agree to the world game. Some say the United States deserved it. They bring evidence that makes me want to push my hands over my ears or cry. I am already crying for human beings who were killed. Everyone is calling everyone else a terrorist. The School of the Americas trained counter insurgency forces that killed hundreds of thousands of people in Guatemala. Sanctions in Iraq have killed that many children. Is that not a great horror? Some say we must break the cycle of retaliation that has dominated geopolitics for four thousand years. Some say violence is a poor way to settle disputes. Some say the way to end war is to stop fighting. Usually the sound of rubber-soled shoes is soft against warm pavement. You walk with friends, hold banners, signs you made the night before at some café. People drive by and honk in support, or shout obscenities out the window. Last Wednesday someone shouted from the window of a commercial truck, *Go back to I-Ran*. I've never been to Iran which is, at the moment, our ally. Usually demonstrations are peaceful. Usually one doesn't think, *Today I will be shot for speaking out, for carrying a sign, for shouting, for setting a piece of cloth on fire*. These are not capital crimes. Always law enforcement personnel hover. Protesters put flowers in gun barrels in the sixties. Our weapons were signs and songs, stoned out imaginations and a deep conviction that war was wrong. Sometimes police will rise up in fear, violence will leap out — in Tiananmen Square, at Kent State, in

Islamabad, in Genoa where international protests against corporate crime incited a police riot. Sometimes they will fire into a crowd. One mind cannot understand all of it. One peace group says, *If you don't think one small voice can have an impact, you have never been bitten by a mosquito.* Somehow from the debris of human conflict, somewhere in a million different agendas for change, somehow in the soft pound of rubber soled shoes on pavement, the rag headed and eternal human face of peace beams like pure starlight, says we must *be* the change we seek. It's strange out here on the street and hard on the ears, but a vast coalition is burgeoning. Every act of resistance is a courageous act. How difficult could it be to get the people of the earth to agree on that one thing — *No more atrocity.*

SB

(*photographs pages 98, 99*)

Ibrihim Al-Mansi With the Key to His Home, 2001, Beit Jala, Palestine. The home was taken from him in 1948.

Grandfather Jabber, 1998, Hebron, Palestine. Israel ran two four-lane highways through their orchards, offering them $60 in compensation. The Jabber family refused the money. They have lost 13 properties to settlement expansion. He is holding a survey to the family property and a deed from the Ottoman Empire.

Ode To *The Onion* (*a found poem*)

America's Finest News Source
September 26, 2001
<onion.com>

"Holy Fucking Shit," the headline reads.

Leading stories include:

"U.S. Vows To Defeat Whoever It Is We Are At War With"

"Arab-American Third-Grader Returns From Recess Crying,
Saying He Didn't Kill Anyone"

"God Angrily Clarifies 'Don't Kill' Rule"

"A Shattered Nation Longs To Care About Stupid Bullshit Again"

"Hijackers Surprised To Find Selves in Hell"

I come across the September 26 issue two months later —
when my sense of humor has sort-of recovered,
remember seeing the "God Angrily Clarifies" article
on the internet in September and thinking it was good —
not funny, just good.

More stories include:

"Bush Sr. Apologizes To Son For Funding Bin Laden In '80s"

"U.S. Urges Bin Laden To Form Nation It Can Attack"

"Area Man Uses WTC Attack As Excuse To Call Ex-Girlfriend"

I spend hours reading alternative news on the internet —
"The Onion" is the first thing that's made me laugh in months,
(and also cry).

SB

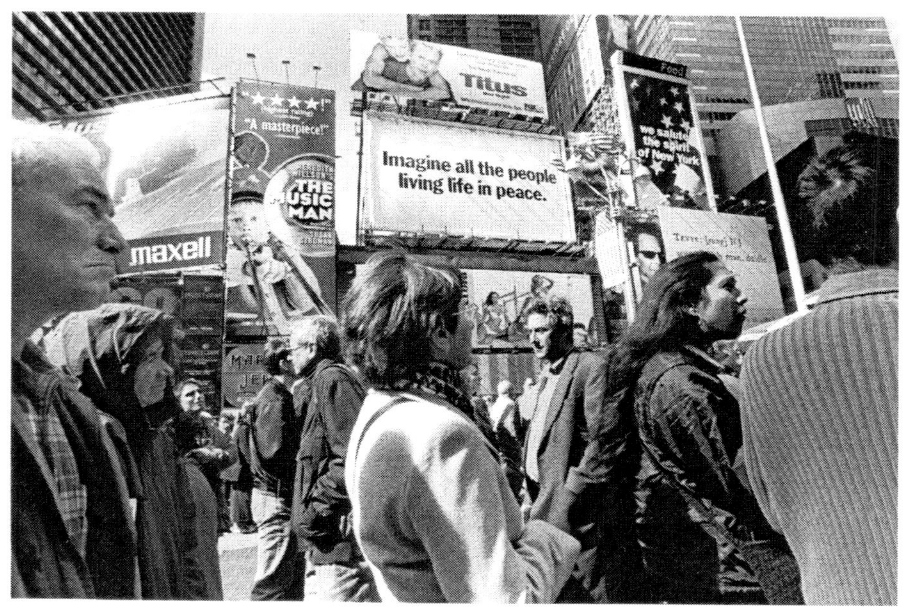

Liberty Street

Toxic dust, debris, and reality blew out of the World Trade Center, charred file folders, a bent photograph of someone's family reunion, pieces of cell phones, scraps of frantic voices saying *I love you*, fax paper, body parts, ghostly white powder, full of asbestos, everybody's desktop. And the layers of our understanding collapsed, covering the reality of one instant ago with small particles of exploded steel, glass, human beings vaporized, the horror of human beings *falling head first out of a nine story gaping hole in the North Tower, one every ten seconds. I turned to help someone who ran out of the elevator, on fire, and turned again to see a body on the street, smashed, in fetal position. It had to have come from the sky*. One man who got out, came down from a floor in the 80s, said they made a floor a minute until around the 30s, when they started meeting firefighters coming up, carrying heavy equipment, gasping for breath. It used to be all right for firefighters to charge into a burning skyscraper to rescue people. It used to be possible to do that. Six people in Irene's family in New York are firefighters, two died, the rest are desolate, wonder how they will endure the searing mask of heroism. When the billowing thick cloud of everything that had been the World Trade Center enveloped Liberty Street and what came to be known as Ground Zero, reality was full of beeping signals. Emergency locators wailed until their batteries ran out. No one could help the ones who lived and died to rescue other human beings, anyone — Christian, Jew, Muslim, Colombian, Chinese, New Yorker, tourists from Ohio. How Ground Zero turned into a shrine then, a shrine alive with steel workers and firemen, police officers, Red Cross rescue workers — singular human forms, dumbstruck, cold and exhausted, grief-stricken and determined to dig their way into a seven story high mass grave to find survivors. How Ground Zero became a shrine of stench and rain and death, a shrine of candles and flowers, cards, posters with the photographs of the missing, *She has a tattoo of a star on her right ankle*. How someone found the tattoo, nothing else. A shrine of American Flags. How the shrine became an epic of compassion that rose out of fire as New Yorkers appeared from all over the city with bottled water and power bars, free massages, clean socks, hot meals, coffee, a place to stay. How Ground Zero was smoldered for three months, how concrete and steel smashed seven stories underground and new pockets of air kept reigniting the fire. How layers and layers of fire leaped out. How every flame had two tongues — a living one full of community and endurance and a death flame ravenous for retaliation. How some screamed for annihilation — *I want whoever did this blown off the planet*. How the government ratcheted up for war. But some said, *No more death. Not in my name. Don't kill any more innocent people in my name*. How Liberty Street remembered the compassion in her name as the firefighter beepers fell silent. How we remembered no one is free until everyone is. How governments rushed off half-cocked to drop bombs on the defenseless and impoverished people of Afghanistan. How all religions condemn war. How there has to be another way or Liberty has no meaning. How America could have remembered the best of her, could have grown determined to fix the worst. How the world's appetite for atrocity reached a swift glut, then opened it's ravenous caw again. How everything happened at once on Liberty Street when layers of vaporized reality cloaked everything we we thought we knew.

SB

(Photograph facing page)
Living Together, Time Square, NYC, October, 2001.

Keys

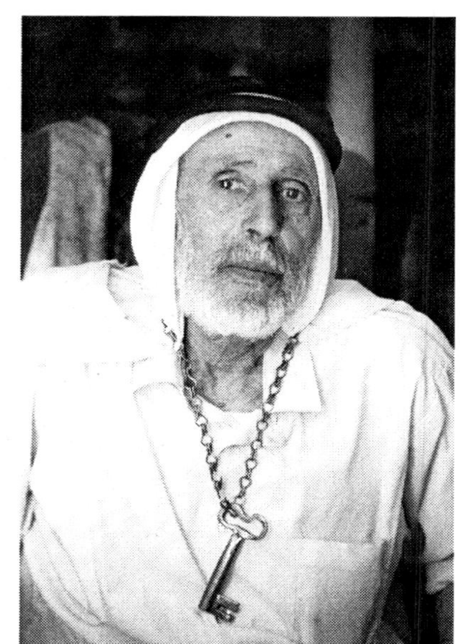

If the earth is alive, then it is sentient,
and scientists will summersault
for the next thousand years as
the masks we call knowledge fall away,
and we try to understand what sort
of creature our living universe
could be, what part of it we are,
perhaps a cancer, or the funny bone,
dust, or an aberrant sort of water.
Perhaps ownership will fall away,
and with it stealing, and with that,
government, and then atrocity.

Perhaps in a kinder world human
beings will draw energy from stars,
from wind, and there will be enough for everyone. Perhaps wealth will be
distributed fairly, and healthcare, and education. Perhaps all children
will have parents who are kind. Perhaps human beings will celebrate
their differences, tolerate strange ideas, and stranger gods.

For now, Grandfather Jabber holds a survey of his land in one hand,
huge muscular hands that have worked the land, know it grain by grain.
In the other hand he holds a deed that is three hundred years old.
A fifty year old treaty pre-empts his deed. They have ordered his house
leveled. Bulldozers will come.

Old men in Palestine wear huge keys around their necks, to symbolize
the homes and land that was taken from them at the end of the last war
by victors intent on planting seeds for the next clash of civilizations
deep into the soul of the earth. There are issues here.
The land belongs to Grandfather Jabber.

The people who now own it are the historical owners of land stolen
in turn from them by people who can't imagine giving holocaust
survivors back their homes, land, property. My country sits on land
stolen from people who did not believe human beings could own
the earth. They thought it was a free and sacred being.

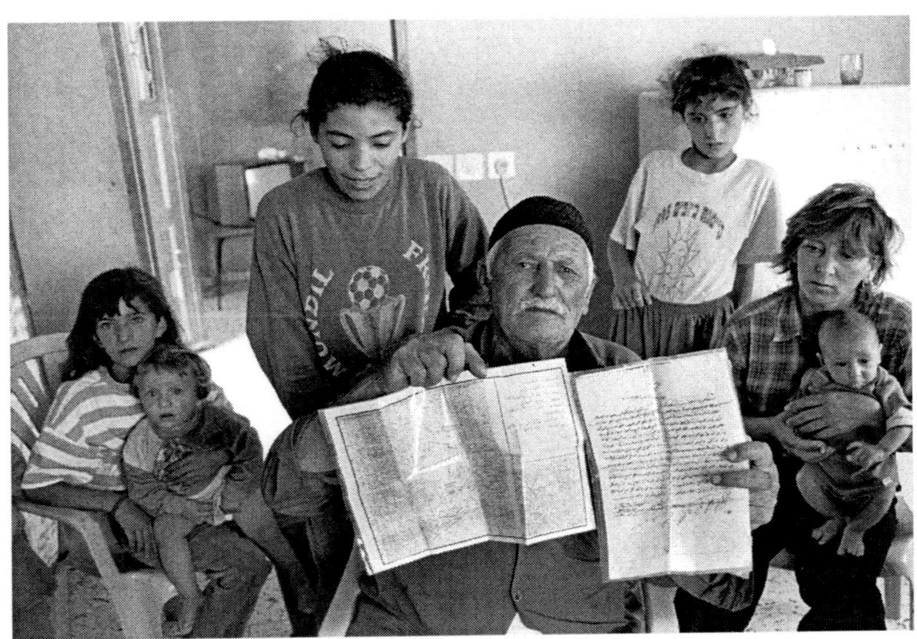

When Time Came to a Standstill...

Aishe hates the present. She doesn't care which present she's living in, she hates it. For her, time stopped in the autumn of 1948 when she fled her village of Zakariya. "It is the most beautiful place on earth," she boasts. "They say Haifa is more beautiful," someone teases. "Haifa, my foot," she retorts. "I'm telling you Zakariya is the best. We had olive trees and fig trees as far as the eye could see. We grew the best tomatoes too. They were big and juicy and I've yet to taste any tomatoes like them."

Once on the subject of Zakariya, nothing can stop Aishe. Most of the time she doesn't even care if anyone is listening. It is as if she enters a trance and is traveling through time. She keeps on talking. "We had an abundant harvest of tomatoes each summer. We couldn't eat them all and that is why we stored them for winter. We would slice them, sprinkle salt on them and put them in the sun to dry. Come winter, we would soak them in water and have fresh tomatoes to eat. Almighty Creator, damn the Israelis and the day we set eyes on them," she sighs.

A single tear gently rolls down Aishe's wrinkled cheek. She wipes it quickly before anyone takes notice. Those who know her well know she is thinking about her son Mohammed. "He was still sucking milk from my breast when we left Zakariya. He wouldn't stop crying. He cried the entire time that we hid in the hills surrounding Zakariya. When we heard that the Jews had entered our village and started our long walk toward Hebron to the southeast, he still continued to cry. Then one midday, he stopped. I thought he was tired and had gone to sleep. When we stopped for the night and I uncovered my breast to feed him, he did not stir. I carried his body in my arms for four days before we finally reached a village in the outskirts of Hebron and his father dug a hole in the grounds of the local cemetery and buried him."

Of the nine children that Aishe bore, only four survived. The rest died sometime in the 1950s when Aishe found herself living in a small tent in what became known as Dheisheh Refugee Camp just outside Bethlehem. An only daughter who had been terribly spoiled by her parents, Aishe was not accustomed to the hardship that was to come. "We came to Dheisheh with nothing except the clothes on our backs. We had no money at all. 'Abdul Fatah had to sell even our camel in Hebron so we could buy food for the children."

Aishe married 'Abdul Fatah when she was 13. "I was a little girl and had no idea what was happening. Because I was their only daughter, my parents did not force me to do any housework and I was always out in the barley fields playing with my girlfriends. After the wedding, I lived with my parents-in-law until it was time for me to bathe," she murmurs.

"You mean you never took a bath before your wedding?" Aishe's young granddaughter asks shyly. "No silly, I am talking about taking my first bath when my first menstrual cycle ended. When I married your grandfather, I wasn't menstruating yet and had to live with his parents for three months until I did. After the first cycle ended and I washed myself, I moved into my husband's house to consummate the marriage."

Aishe never loved 'Abdul Fatah. She never forgave him for marrying her at such a tender age. To this day, she insists that he was 36 years old when they married. "How could he have been 36 when he died at the age of 88 in 1984, mother?" her son Mahmoud shouts angrily. "He was 26 when he married you." But Aishe refuses to listen. "He was an old man and had no business marrying a young child like me," she insists.

Aishe's resentment of 'Abdul Fatah is not uncharacteristic of her. She hates everything in her life. She hates being a refugee, she hates the Jordanians for ruling the West Bank, she hates the Israelis and their occupation. She hates everything that happened to her after that fateful autumn in 1948 and no one can say or do anything to make her change her mind. For her, time came to a standstill when she walked out of Zakariya and it will never go into motion again until she can go back.

"I insist on my right of return and will never accept compensation instead," Aishe says feverishly. "I want to go back to my land." And Aishe knows exactly where her land is. She keeps all the yellowish and tattered land deeds inside a small tin container. Dated back to the 1930s, the land deeds specify the boundaries of each piece of land that 'Abdul Fatah owned. "Read this and see for yourself," says Aishe as she unfolds one of the land deeds and sticks it in her grandson's face. The boy laughs. "But grandmother, Zakariya doesn't look the same anymore. How can you tell where your land is?" The boy reads out loud. "Witnesses signing this document testifies that 'Abdul Fatah bought a piece of land on this date. The land is located between the wheat field of Abu Saleh and Abu Salman. Abu Saleh's fig trees mark the land's northern boundary while Abu Salman's well marks the southern boundary."

The boy tries to explain to his grandmother that Zakariya has been transformed in the past 50 years and that it is impossible to identify the family's property. Aishe angrily snatches the deed out of his hand and puts away. "I know exactly where the land is," she screams at him. "All they have to do is take me there and I'll show them. I haven't gone senile yet."

Aishe shoos the grandchildren out of the room. "They think I'm going to give it up just like that," she mumbles out loud. "For 50 years I have held onto these deeds and they think I'm going to give it up." Then, almost in wail, she starts. "I had to walk for miles on end to gather wood and sell it for peanuts in order to feed my children. They think it is easy being a refugee. I didn't ask to be a refugee. I didn't ask to live with thousands of other people in one damn square kilometer. There is no air to breathe here in Dheisheh. All the air is in Zakariya. We had a nice breeze even on the hottest of days."

Just as suddenly as she started talking, Aishe stops. Minutes later, everyone in the house can hear her cry. It is a muffled and choked sound. "Stop, grandmother," begs her granddaughter. "I swear to God Almighty that we'll go back. We are from Zakariya and we must go back." Aishe doesn't answer and the girl knows better than to push her luck.

As the children go outside to play, Aishe starts singing a sad melody, making up the words as she goes. "O, my son Mohammed, where are you? Why don't you come and see what has become of me? O, my son Mohammed, if only you were here. You would be a grown man now and maybe an engineer. O, my son Mohammed, I held you in my arms. My milk was waiting for you, but may God forgive you, you did not open your eyes."

MH

Palestine Report, 1 May 1998

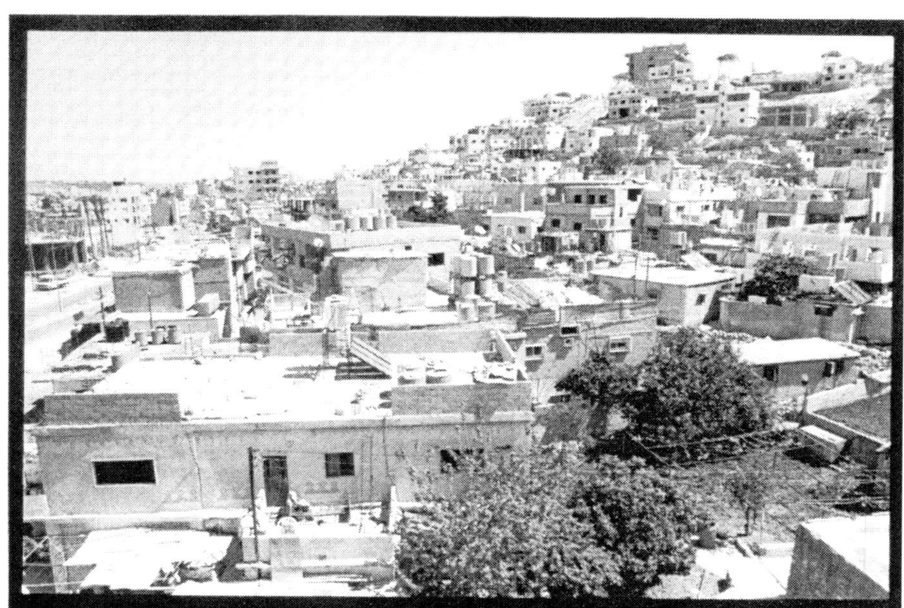

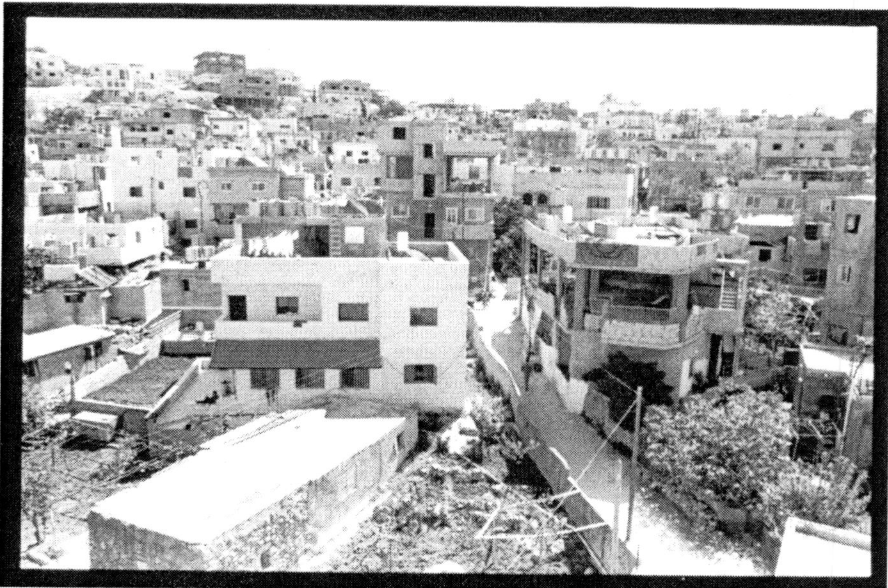

Dheisheh Refugee Camp, 2001, Palestine. Bethlehem, Beit Jala and Bet Sahour are across a small valley from Jersalem. Everything is so close and yet partitioned so people have to wait in long check point lines to go from place to place.

AP

Dheisheh Refugee Camp

I lived just off the surface of the second photograph — to the right, up hill. On the left is the main road. Israel built a six foot high barb wire fence around us. There was a revolving steel gate you had to pass through to get in or out. It was too small for a person and their groceries. They had a fort on the top of the hill, flashed a giant spotlight through the streets at night to enforce the curfew. If someone heard soldiers, or if the light was coming, you could duck into any house and the people would hide you. Even if soldiers came into the house and beat people, they wouldn't tell where you were. Soldiers could come into your house anytime they wanted to. People think — how could you live like this, but they don't understand. I love this place. I love these people. It was the warmest family I have ever known. I won't be happy until I go back. Muna is speaking. She is a Palestinian/American who lived in this refugee camp just outside of Jerusalem for ten years. *Jerusalem is right over there behind the trees on the left side of the picture. I couldn't go there. We were in a cage. At first, in 1949 they built a small one room box for each family. You can see two of them at the bottom of the picture. It didn't matter how many there were in your family — twelve or twenty, everyone got the same space for cooking, for living. I can't go back. They told me that when I left last year. I am dangerous because I speak and write in English. I saw an old woman with a huge plastic bowl of vegetables balanced on her head. A nineteen-year-old soldier knocked her down. The vegetables rolled down the hill. These people will not back down. The next day the old woman went back to the market. From my window, I watched her carry her food past this same young man again.* Later Muna talks to my son about antique Mustangs, and because he is a twin, she shows him pictures of her sister's twin boys. Later, my son tells me the old Mustang he bought for $500 and sold a month later for $450 represents his freedom. Now he says he'll be an underwater welder. He shows her a picture of his brother. Her husband, Maan, *explains to me the history of the poet Enhueduenna*— pronounced *Andwanna*. I asked her to tell me about Alan's photograph, *Can you show me where you lived?* I said. We know so little about the Middle East, we must listen with depth to what Muna is able to say.

SB, MH

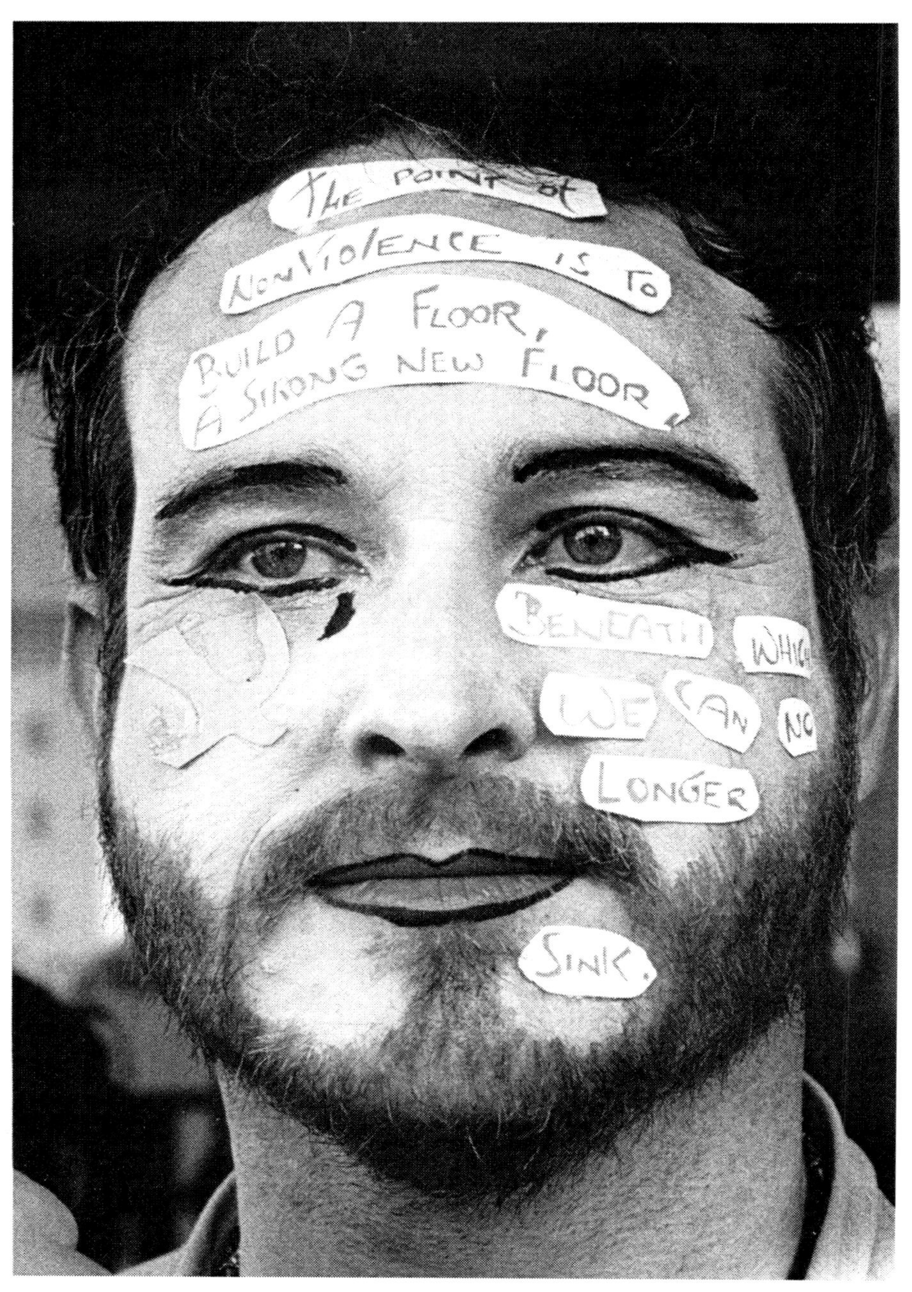

Gay Texans Agains the War, 1974, Austin, TX.

AP

Don't Label Me

Or if you do label the lines around my eyes —
forgiveness, read along the inside of my eyelids
the dream that flew through me last night.
I can't remember it but you should be able to,
if you try hard enough, we *are* the dreamtime.

Don't label me —
blonde, a woman, feminist, mother, wife, pacifist.
Label the sound of my fingers hitting computer keys,
the knack I have of seeing to the core,
or all I miss because I am too thick to flow inside
your mind. I'd go there if I could.

Label the poem that keeps leaping out of me,
the song I can't quite find the notes for,
it is your song too. Do you recall the melody?

Label the question marks that fly from my fingertips,
the photographs that click past so quickly only the finest
lense can hold the textured black and white of seeing
what of us is worth keeping, our humanity and dignity,
the man, the woman each is capable of being.

Label the unknowable question of us,
how one walks along the creek to find peace,
how another swims or creates music,
how anyone with sense would rather hold a baby
soft from sleep or laughing than be famous.

Label the simple humanity we share that makes us holy.
Write *peace* across my face.

SB

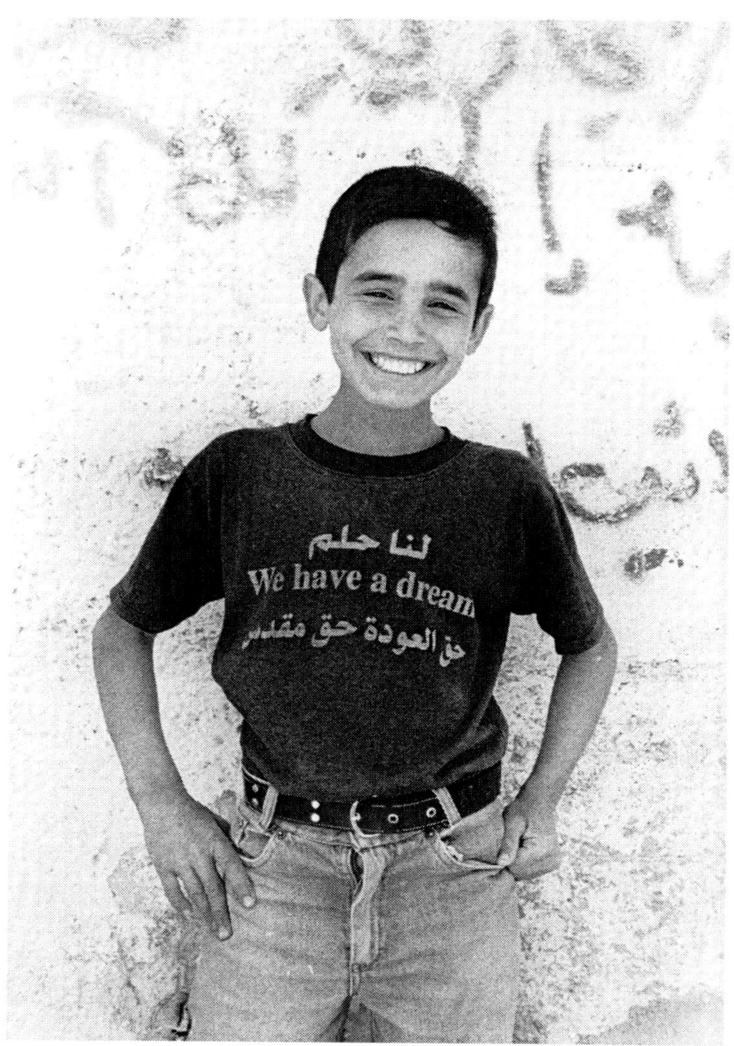

We Have a Dream, Dheisheh Refugee Camp, 2001.

AP

I fool myself into thinking that I am happy here because I am free. But I know I am not happy because my people aren't free. Freedom is a birth-right, yet it has been denied the Palestinians for nearly 54 years. Wake up you sleepy world. Israel's occupation of the Palestinians has gone on far too long. The time to end it is now, so all our children can live in freedom.

MH

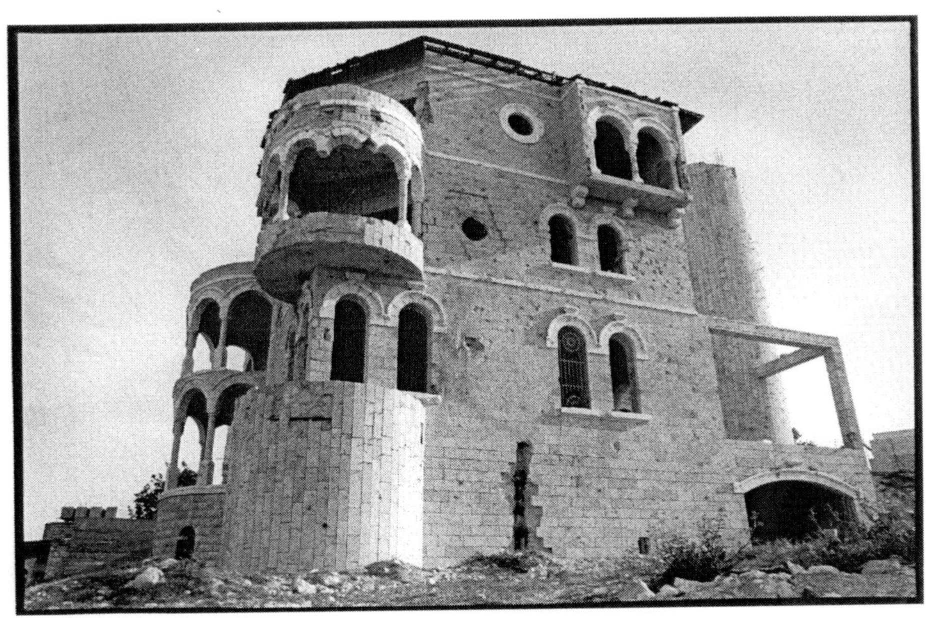

Dream Castle/Nightmare, 2001, Beit Jala, Palestine. The person who built this house has lived for many years in El Salvador sending money back to Palestine in order to construct his dream home. Now it has been destroyed. Yet he has never set foot in it. He has refused compensation from the Palestinian Authority, preferring that the money go to those in greater need. A grand gesture. Peace could start here.

AP

This is the house in Beit Jala from which ***The Hole*** photograph comes. We now see the hole from the other side. Today this home was on the morning news. As war again ravages the people of Palestine and Israel, I am profoundly moved by this world scale illustration of how victims of violence and abuse become perpetrators. There must be time for healing, respite from these cycles of retaliation. Peace could start here.

12/01/01, SB

Afterword: Letter to Everyone
(10/13/01)

In these tragic, imponderable and dangerous times I find myself saying over and over again, "There is no substitute for goodwill."

I find myself wanting to reach out to family, friends, to the writers, artists, activists I have had the privilege to work with and know. I want to say, "I am proud to know you." I send love and condolence to everyone who has lost loved ones in these tragic events.

I have gone from shock to tears in the midst of which I realize I don't want another innocent person to die as a result of this atrocity.

I was born at the end of W.W.II. In my lifetime, in spite of my (our) dissent, the United States has pursued economic and political policies that have alienated much of the world and caused enormous destruction, loss of life and environmental degradation.

I believe violence is a poor way to settle disputes, have come to understand that only justice can manifest peace, that every act of violence is "retaliation" in the eye of the perpetrator.

Shall we strike back at, for example, Afghanistan?

The women of Afghanistan are among the most oppressed people on the planet. Are they to answer in blood for the actions (despicable actions) of multi-millionaire international terrorists who vow to kill Americans for behaviors many of us have condemned for decades? For the actions of a government which keeps women in a narrow, hopeless prison? A government over which they have zero influence?

Be kind to someone today.

Shall we strike at every country in which terrorists cells have existed, exist? That would be perhaps 50 countries. The perpetrator is a stealth, multi-national network, corporation, if you will, not a country, not an alliance of nations. Terrorism is a dark force, born of grim realities.

War is a conflict between governments. Pearl Harbor was an attack on one government by another government. That is not what has occurred. War is an irrelevant response.

Be kind to someone today.

America has been violated, civilians have been massacred. The world has been violated. How shall we respond to this atrocity?

We must be strong, vigilant and just.

On a local NPR program a Muslim woman named Maria said she felt a deep shame and sorrow for her people — only a fraction of a percent of whom support terrorism which she said comes from a deep human flaw. I feel shame too for the actions of my people — the ones who hoard money, power, influence — the hegemon which has behaved so badly in the world.

The transformation of a public transportation system into weapons of mass destruction is a re-definition of the concept of war that makes our weapon systems irrelevant and re-defines power as dangerously as did the advent of the atomic bomb.

We would do well to consider alternatives. We would do well to be kind to one another. There is no substitute for goodwill.

Be kind to someone today.

I love this country, and the people in it. Can we find the wisdom to transform this horrible reality? We are people capable of diversity.

What if we said we would follow a rule of law. And did it.

What if we called for a world treaty against terrorism? Violators answerable to a world court.

Alternately, what if we mobilize for conventional war, send our men and women across the planet to massacre people who had nothing to do with the atrocity — would that not leave us uniquely open to anything terrorists want to perpetrate? Would that not leave us as vulnerable as the undeveloped nations have been to the machinations of multi-national corporations and their political arms which — along with the seeds scattered at the end of WWII — have created the context from which these atrocities arise. Would that not be recruiting for terrorists? What is really going on here?

Would it not be better to be vigilant, and just?

Be kind to someone today.

911 — America is changed from this day forth. Can we lead the world away from another cycle of massive retaliation, away from the first war of the 21st century and toward a rule of law, international law. With teeth.

America was the target of this atrocity, but so was world commerce — the World Trade Center and Wall Street. 911 was a direct hit to multi-national business. We know these corporations need regulation. Many people advocate, not random violence, but a rule of law — transparency, the end of the limited liability corporation.

If valid international law does not yet exist, we must create it. Or will this be a century of chaos, the cure for which will drastically curtail the freedoms which are central to our way of life?

What is just for individual human beings is good for the world. There is no substitute for goodwill.

Be kind to someone today.

Susan Bright, 10/13/01

About the Writers

Susan Bright is the author of nineteen books of poetry, three of which (**Far Side of the Word, Tirades And Evidence Of Grace** and **House of the Mother**) have been recipients of Austin Book Awards. **Tirades And Evidence Of Grace** also won the Violet Crown Award. She is the editor of Plain View Press which since 1975 has published one-hundred-and-thirty-five books. Her work as a poet, publisher, activist and educator has taken her all over the United States and abroad. In Texas she has received a proclamation from the Senate honoring her literary and community work, and in Austin she received the Woman of the Year Award in 1990 from the local Women's Political Caucus. Her last book, **Breathing Under Water**, is written in the voice of a community of people who are swimmers and who work to preserve the Edwards aquifer. Susan is the mother of twin boys, a year around lap swimmer, an environmental activist and an advodate for peace.

Muna Hamzeh is a Palestinian-American journalist who's been writing about Palestinian affairs since 1985. She is the author of **Refugees in Our Own Land: Chronicles From a Palestinian Refugee Camp in Bethlehem** (Pluto Press, September 2001) and a contributing writer in **The New Intifada: Resisting Israel's Apartheid** (Verso Books, September 2001). In the mid 1980s, Hamzeh wrote about the Palestinian issue from Washington, DC. At the end of 1988, she moved to Palestine, where she lived in Dheisheh Refugee Camp in Bethlehem and continued her work as a journalist. Over the years, Hamzeh's articles on Palestinian affairs have appeared in ***Middle East International*** (London), the ***Jerusalem Quarterly File*** (Jerusalem), ***Palestine Report*** (Jerusalem), ***Ha'aretz*** (Tel Aviv), ***Jerusalem Star*** (Amman), ***The Economist*** (London), ***Ad-Dustour*** (Amman), ***al-Fajr English Weekly***(Jerusalem), the ***Christian Science Monitor*** (Boston), ***Jerusalem Repor***t (Jerusalem), the ***Muslim*** (Islamabad), ***The Saudi Gazette*** (Riyadh), ***New Outlook Magazine*** (Tel Aviv), ***The Link*** (Washington), ***The Austin Chronicle***, ***BBC-Online*** and a score of other publications. In Austin, she works for the Austin Civil Rights Project.

About the Photographer

For over thirty years, since 1968, **Alan Pogue** has been photographing social and political movements in Texas and around the world. The focus of Alan's work includes migrant laborers, prison conditions and criminal justice, Cuba, culture and conflict in the Middle East, and Iraq under sanctions as well as other topics centered on efforts of peace and social betterment.

Alan began his career as a photographer while serving as a chaplin's assistant and combat medic in Vietnam. His photos have appeared in several national and international publications including the ***New York Times Magazine, The Boston Globe, The Washington Post, The L.A. Times, The Austin American Statesman, The Dallas Morning News, Kyodo News Japan,*** *and* ***Texas Monthly.*** Alan has also served as staff photographer for the ***Texas Observer*** for 29 years.

Alan's many honors include a Dobie-Paisano fellowship and being named Austin's "Best Photographer" by the ***Austin Chronicle*** ten years running, 1990-1999. His work has been widely exhibited nationally and internationally. In 1989 Alan's National Farmworker show, sponsored by the National Center for Farmworker Health, was shown in the Cannon House office building in Washington, D.C. In 1995 Alan was invited to present his work on border issues in North America at an international conference at The Sorbonne. In 1998, at the request of C.U.R.E. (Citizens United for the Rehabilitation of Errants), and with the help of a grant from Resist, Alan produced a nationwide show on prison reform that opened in 1999 at the Washington Center for Photography. (see attached article from the December 1999 issue of Photo District News)

Alan recently returned from Iraq where he worked with Veteran's For Peace in a campaign to repair water treatment facilities and raise international awareness of the suffering caused by U.S./U.N. sanctions. An exhibit from his ongoing work with Voices In the Wilderness is touring nationally.

Alan Pogue uses the camera as a humanitarian instrument to promote mercy and understanding.

Stuart Heady, ***The Good Life***, December 2001